My Sleeveless Heart:
Lyrical Memoirs of a Naked Soul

Joshua DuBois

DEDICATION

I dedicate this book to all the women that I have ever had the privilege of sharing time with on this planet. Be you family, friend, fiancé, fan, fling, foe or forgotten, your involvement in my life is what has transformed me into the man I am today

CONTENTS

Introduction   1

Chapter 1: Attraction   6

Chapter 2: Desire   15

Chapter 3: Pursuit   23

Chapter 4: Conquest   30

Chapter 5: Captivation   40

Chapter 6: Fulfillment   48

Chapter 7: Attachment   56

Chapter 8: Dedication   63

Chapter 9: Miscommunication   71

Chapter 10: Unappreciation   79

Chapter 11: Severance   88

Chapter 12: Forgiveness   97

Exercise Appendix   107

Lyrical Memoirs: Sex   124

Lyrical Memoirs: Love   136

Lyrical Memoirs: Fear   147

ACKNOWLEDGMENTS

I give all glory to God for the completion of this book and I know that He watched over me with the spirit and protection of my ancestors.

For an entire lifetime of love and support with all of my creative endeavors, I thank the DuBois family Gary DuBois, Sharon DuBois, Jordan DuBois and Jarred DuBois. To embody the prestige of our heritage and enrich the esteem of our legacy is an honor and a privilege that you all have given me the courage to accept. I love you all, thank you.

To my line brother, advisor, biggest supporter and dearest friend Michael Mallery I thank you for taking the time to guide me and turn me into a man that sometimes I can't even see. This book was entirely inspired by you and it became my greatest work to date. I appreciate your unwavering support and when this book is an international best-seller, I'll be in the lead for our race to the top… so take that LB.

To Sheree Lyne Pitts, I thank you for being my mirror. Thank you for showing me everything that holds me back and bringing me to my own attention so that I can change my life. Thank you for tearing down my walls, shaking me up, shattering my ego a little bit, breaking my heart open just enough so that new light can get in. Thank you for being my soulmate.

To my gentlemen mentors Darryl Barnes, Corey Yeager, Michael Firven, Ben Sheffield, James Smith and Gabriel Abdelaziz I thank you for setting such an amazing example of what it means to love a woman by loving yourself. You gentlemen listened to me in my many stages of youthful ignorance and confusion and guided me in the right direction with the perceptions I needed to transform into a supportive, fair and compatible partner.

To my female friends/counselors Erica Harris, Nneka Egbuniwe, Sharonda Cannon, Shamanicka Boykins, Avery Kemp and Wendi Vaughn I thank you for your patience and faith that I would someday realize how irrational my perception of women was. You are the examples of what a woman is supposed to be in our generation and I appreciate you for mending my brokenness and opening my eyes to the beauty of love. To Schante Harding my dear friend I thank you for being such a helpful reflection of myself by not only teaching me that I can genuinely love but that I am worthy of love from someone so wonderful.

To my boys (to men) Desmond Cole, Kenrick Pete and Chad Morton I thank you for reminding me of my own potential by simply showing me yours. Your efforts and hard working natures motivate me to continue to pursue what it is that makes me feel like I can do anything. I thank you for being there with me through the best and the worst of times. Even though most of it could have been avoided if I had been a more complete version of myself, I thank you gents for sticking with me and helping me find him. To my Chipps Matthew Marshall, Cody Canyon and Noah Sanderson I thank you for all that time on the bus from city to city in Europe, in our rooms with salami and ananas pizza and sweating all over the marley during pre-show Insanity (respectively) talking about our romantic interests; what makes us tick; how things are going with our loves back home; how we can improve ourselves as men to be better suited to love ourselves and thusly share that love with the rest of the world including our mates. To my Chipps Joey Pena, Jeffrey Garrovillo and Curtis Haines, I thank you boys for those late nights up at the hotel bar, dirt cheap bottles of Disaronno and blind navigated walks to and from the gym (respectivey) talking about our love and touches back home; the stupid fights with a girlfriend and how to avoid them; how to make someone that's not ready for forever realize their value. This book wouldn't have been the same without all the years I've spent learning from each and every one of you. Thank you so much.

To my webmistresses Amber Jex and Tracey Lincoln I thank you for your tireless efforts in the creation of my website, promotional paraphernalia and front and back covers for this book. I had the vision, but you ladies made it possible to share that vision with the professionalism and style that I expect from any of my numerous adventures. To Cody Canyon and Laura Ferguson I thank you for the cover of this book. I was inspired to transform this book from a simple compilation of my poems and song lyrics to the completely open and honest expression of myself and my ideas. This picture captures and fully expresses the essence and message of this book.

Introduction

If there can be any lesson learned by anyone who has read books about the opposite sex (or the same sex if preferred) and dealing with them romantically it's that these books can only give general information about what might be going on in the mind of someone you are interested in. None of these books can tell you exactly what to do in certain situations in your love life, they just give good ideas. These works written by scientists, behaviorists, psychologists and other experts compile data from hundreds to thousands of people, but that data does you no good when you try to apply their generic advice to your loved one in particular.

Following general advice based on nonspecific information is only successful a fraction of the time. Even circumstance specific advice has a tendency to backfire. Ask yourself how many times someone has come to you with a problem that you dealt with before and you told them exactly what you did to fix the situation. Now ask yourself how differently their results were compared to yours. Go even farther and think of a time when you were having a problem that a friend, family member or peer had already solved and you did exactly what they did in your situation. Most likely neither situation turned out exactly the same. Why is this?

Well, every person in the world is an individual with his or her own thoughts, background experiences, opinions, fears and beliefs. One thing that makes us uniquely human is that we are all different. If everyone is different, then we are actually dehumanizing the people we love when we react to them the same way another person would; especially if our reaction is based on how to react to somebody else that isn't our loved one. I must clarify that I do not oppose these books by any means because they shed very interesting light on love and relationships based on years of trial and error, scientific study and personal experiences.

Books such as *The Male Brain* and *The Female Brain* both written by Louann Brizendine, M.D, *Brain Sex* written by Anne Moir, Ph.D. and David Jessel and *The Art of Seduction* written by Robert Greene are all exceptionally enlightening and very informative but we must take it upon ourselves not to just perform the actions we read about, but understand ourselves and apply the behaviors necessary to have fulfilling and long lasting relationships.

As many of you know, everyone on the entire planet thinks they are an expert on relationships. Throughout our romantic lives, our friends, families, co-workers, mentors, associates, peers, heroes and enemies alike all seem to know a little something about what to do in a romantic encounter or predicament. I don't want to become just another wrong answer or poor piece of advice to follow so I want to take this time to hit you with the DISCLAIMER that this book and all of its contents are strictly the portrayal of my thoughts, ideas, observations and life experiences in dealing with relationships.

I have been an attentive watcher of people since childhood and my position in life continues to be the listening ear of a counselor. I have developed several unique theories, beliefs and approaches that I consistently use when I am approached with a question or dilemma regarding a relationship or romantic encounter. This book is simply the compilation of these theories and practices explained in the sequence that relationships occur from introduction to break-up and everything that happens thereafter. To enhance my explanation, my thoughts are accompanied by poems that I have written out of the same scenarios.

The story of my romantic life is far from over and I have made my share of mistakes just like everyone else has. As an adult I have given myself the opportunity to own up to those mistakes and evolve into a better man with each passing day. I make sure that I connect with myself and my personal reasons why I want to change. Many times we try to change ourselves to fit in or to satisfy others but those alterations are temporary. In this book I plan on describing every detail of my thought process as it pertains to my involvement in relationships.

My goal is to inspire everyone to keep their mind open and their priorities in continuous evaluation for the happiest life possible; whether involved in a relationship or not. The format of this book is based on the idea that the "significant other" I talk about will remain the same throughout the entire book. That way I am able to discuss what happens in a relationship from start to finish and use the same scenario throughout the book.

Everyone in the world is entitled to his or her opinion and I am humbled and grateful that all of you have given me your time so that I can share mine. Our society has become so focused on the fleeting aspects of life that it is rare to simply sit down and have a genuine conversation. Share your fears, hopes, dreams and opinions truthfully and unfiltered. I must warn you, though, as stated before I am not giving any advice on relationships nor am I giving a specific course of action to take because everyone's scenarios are different from everyone else's.

The hypothetical relationship that I describe in this book is just that. Hypothetical. Even if your life does not line up with the scenarios I describe, just keep reading. At some point, you will be able to directly identify with at least part of the examples I give either in your own life or in the life of a friend or family member. *My Sleeveless Heart: Lyrical Memoirs of a Naked Soul* is my contribution to a conversation that we all have every day of our lives whether we know it or not. This conversation is based on a question with an ever-changing answer that will never truly be understood… what is love?

Phase 1

Sex

1

Attraction

Hypothetically imagine the best you on your best day. Your mood is just right, your responsibilities have been taken care of and you are in public in a place that you enjoy. Let's say you are sitting at a bar in your most flattering outfit, walking through the gym with a tantalizing glisten of sweat, leaning casually against your shopping cart at the grocery store, earnestly reading an interesting novel at a library or lovingly feeding the birds at the park when you notice that the most beautiful person you have ever seen is walking in your direction.

No matter how calm, cool or collected you were before, the entire world around you collapses into darkness, time seems to slow down, your heart begins to beat faster and the palms of your hands begin to sweat as the focal point of your full attention is now entirely on this person's approach. This arousing reaction to the people we find ourselves attracted to is based in our primitive brain recognizing the likelihood of that person being a potential bearer of children, a suitable protector or quite simply, a proficient sexual partner.

Although this generality is definitely accurate on a wide scale, we must go deeper into not only how our brains react to people that we are attracted to, but why our *minds* find these people attractive (the brain is automatic and reactive and dictates what we do because it is hard-wired to do so but the mind thinks, feels and allows us to make decisions based on our beliefs and experiences instead of our biology). What is it that makes us look at this person with such interest and intrigue without knowing the slightest thing about them? One speculation is that all people have a certain type that we are particularly attracted to. That image is directly linked with old feelings and memories associated with someone that looks like our hypothetically approaching crush.

Everyone's backgrounds differ from socioeconomic status to religious affiliation all the way to the racial demographics of where we grew up. If we look back at the finer details of the people that we have dealt with romantically in our lives it is highly likely that the people we found ourselves attracted to had similar attributes and characteristics as the person with the highest influence in our young life that matches the gender our sexual orientation prefers. Those of us that date women who struggle with monogamy, experienced some sort of sexual assault, grew up with relationship issues with her father, etc. most likely had a strong relationship with a woman with a similar background story. Those of us that date men who have problems with commitment, identity issues (be they sexual or personal), a lack of ambition and drive to better themselves, etc. most likely grew up influenced by a man that has nearly identical personal complications.

With this in mind, we also have to consider the fact that this pattern of personality attraction usually results in these people having physical and behavioral similarities as well. The people that we involve ourselves with usually remind us of the people that had the greatest effect on our lives and the way we perceive the gender of our affections.

My mother and father raised me in the city of Inglewood, CA; an urban city in Los Angeles County. My mother is incredibly intelligent, stunningly beautiful, powerfully opinionated, delicately compassionate and conscientiously honest. In my eyes, she is the type of woman that I wish every man could have the opportunity to meet, experience personally or simply talk to. I have seen first hand the man that her dominant feminine energy can make out of someone. It should be no surprise that the vast majority of women that I have involved myself with share so many of her characteristics.

They all represented loving and supporting comfort to encourage me when the world was at my neck, strong logical sensibilities to help me differentiate the important from the insignificant, unyielding moral values to ensure that I respect myself as well as her and the affection of a mother that let me know they would be compatible mates to raise children with. Being so highly influenced by a woman of these characteristics conditioned my mind to search for these same characteristics in the people I wanted to be with, but there is a problem. How could I have known these women were like my mother before we met? It seems that we register what we know about our influence's (my mother in this instance) characteristics and associate it with the easiest way to recognize them; sight. This is why all the women I have dealt with not only act like my mother, but they look like her too.

On a subconscious level, we register memories of our world with the way that our senses perceive the world around us. When our senses process an experience, that registration activates and the memory, along with the feelings associated with it, springs forth. Back to our hypothetical, the only sense that we are able to use at this point is the sense of sight. If we instinctively seek someone that reminds us of someone we are familiar with or were highly influenced by, it is only natural that we will seek physical attributes that remind us of the characteristics we are already looking for.

In Inglewood, CA I was put through educational institutions that were all focused on providing a top-notch education and black students at a minimum of 95% populated them all. My mother's influence in my home along with the influence of the extremely intelligent and beautiful black women surrounding me throughout my entire educational career created my preference for darker toned black women. My celebrity crushes Serena Williams,

Gabrielle Union, Kerry Washington, Kelly Rowland and Naomi Campbell, to name a few, all have close similarities in physical stature and they all remind me of the attributes I previously mentioned about my mother and the women I have involved myself with.

In *Woman of my Dreams* I start the poem with, "We've never met each other before but I recognize you." This turn of phrase holds meaning in two layers. On one hand I am trying to romantically convince a young lady that I see her as the woman I envision myself marrying and having children with, but there is a deeper meaning. I am letting her know that she falls into the category of women that, to me, represent the values, morals, intellect and beauty that I look for in a long-term partner. Not everyone lives by these rules because there are those that do not have a consistency in the type of person that they date.

Whenever a person cannot find consistency in a particular aspect of their life, they are likely going through a transitional phase where they are trying to figure out what exactly they want from that aspect of life or they are operating with an ulterior motive. In figuring out what we want romantically, men and women both go through the same confusion, but in opposing ways. Men always know *what* we want but have a difficult time figuring out *when* we want it. Conversely, women always know *when* they want something but have the same difficulty deciding *what* exactly they want.

From a man's perspective, he is certain whether or not

he wants his mate to be dainty, bold, daring, promiscuously open-minded, shy, reclusive, etc. These characteristics are developed over time and we normally seek them out and even when we find suitable candidates, we will lie, cheat and deceive them because although he has *what* he wants, that person might not be *what* he is looking for *at the time.* How many men do you know have gone through numerous relationships with significant others that fit his personality and seemed to be perfectly happy but out of nowhere did something to sabotage the relationship? This happens because our instincts to be the hunter and the provider cause us to question the validity of our relationships at the time they are happening. Up until the magic moment that we mature into a man that is willing to accept the responsibility of commitment to one person, many of us go through a large part of life unwilling to settle.

How many women do you know are constantly sharing their desire to be in a long-term relationship but seem to always find something wrong with every man that they date and always change the type of man they give the opportunity to be Mr. Right? I believe this happens because women evolve so significantly and so frequently that they are more willing to sample a wider variety of personality types and physical make-ups to determine which combination is best suited to satisfy her wants and needs. Although she may be ready to find the ideal candidate to sweep her off her feet into happily ever after, the suitors that she encounters may not be suited to satisfy her constantly fluctuating priorities.

The other aspect of being unable to settle on one personality type comes from having something to prove or from withholding an ulterior motive. These motives can come from an infinite list of reasons, but a few of the most frequently experienced include: the desire to seek revenge, a need for variety and an interest in something forbidden or unfamiliar. Revenge is usually sought to exact justice for the offenses committed by an oppressive figure. A wealthy father that does not approve of befriending those from a lower socioeconomic status could cause their son or daughter to focus only on finding a partner of lower financial standing leaving every other characteristic completely up to chance.

The need for variety is normally attributed to those that are more accustomed to associating with people of many different cultures and diversities. A military brat of mixed races that has lived in over 20 different places and speaks 3 languages is much more likely to date people from different backgrounds that match one of the many different standards they developed growing up. I will share a personal story to illustrate the desire for the unfamiliar.

Although I grew up around mostly black women, I have always had a thing for red headed white women as well. This stems from the love for music that I have had since I was a little boy which got exploited when I was six years old watching *Who Framed Roger Rabbit*. Jessica Rabbit singing her enchanting jazz rendition of Peggy Lee's "Why Don't you Do Right" is what made an exception to my preference so if I were to ever date outside my type spectrum, she would probably look like the "Marvel Avengers" Scarlett Johansson, the "That 70s Show" Laura Prepon or the "Easy A" Emma Stone.

There are many different reasons that can explain why we find ourselves attracted to certain people. Whether we understand these reasons or not, we have to acknowledge and embrace them because they are the foundation of the first part of any romantic interaction or potential relationship. If you went to your favorite restaurant for a meal, you more than likely know exactly what you want to eat because you had that dish before. You would not waste your money on something you know you wouldn't like right?

In this case, time is money and all of us are sitting down to eat at the restaurant of love. The "menu" options have some dishes that will tickle your taste buds, some that will burn your pallet and even some that you are extremely allergic to. You have to know what you like and what you can eat so that you can have a pleasant dining experience and not waste your money.

In terms of love, your past experiences should be able to give you an accurate view of how to approach the "menu" in the future whether that means you want your favorite dish with some different ingredients or you just want to eat something else. See **Exercise 1** in the appendix for a few thought provoking ideas to consider and questions to ask yourself about the history of your love life. Hopefully you can begin to understand where you've been romantically and compare that to where you want to go in your life to try and line those goals up with one another.

Let's go back to our hypothetical. That special someone walking up to you at the bar, on the park bench or in the library finally reaches his or her destination… you. You are told that you give off a very intriguing vibe and that it would be so much fun if you would join him or her for lunch. You are asked for your name and even though you respond without making a total fool out of yourself, all you want to do is freeze this moment in time because you know this is the story you will be telling your friends and grandchildren. You've caught their eye, but what are you going   to   do   to   keep   their   attention?

2

Desire

At this very moment you are engaged in a conversation with the man or woman of your dreams. You've learned each other's name, shared interesting tidbits about yourselves, broken the ice with a funny or witty comment and you have fully immersed yourself in the presence of this wonderful person. In this moment, the most important thing in the world is to make sure that your conversation lasts as long as it possibly can. Sadly this is never the case. There is no possible way for us to harness the powerful magic of the first conversation with someone that we find ourselves genuinely attracted to or interested in.

What is it that makes us want to keep this feeling going for as long as possible? We naturally develop a sense of comfort and attachment toward the things that we enjoy and that make us feel good. However, before we find ourselves in moments like these where we find it difficult to end the conversation at an appropriate moment we must find out what part within us makes it hard to walk away for now.

Every person wants and equally wants to be wanted and accepted, however, many times in our lives we experience the feeling of rejection in some way or another. It is through the opposing relationship between rejection and acceptance that we find ourselves so deeply engaged in that first conversation we never want to end. This opposing relationship is not to imply that the only reason we want to keep that first conversation going is to not feel rejected, but to convey how amazing the feeling of acceptance is.

Being able to talk to someone who seems like they have known you your entire life is exhilarating and extremely rare. Since these moments don't last, our minds develop defense mechanisms that try to make sure that we can have moments like them again. The most consistently developed defense is an anxiety to continue talking for as long as possible along with a sense of urgency to end the conversation at a point where we feel successful in our contribution to the conversation.

Although it seems difficult to feel an extreme urgency to prolong something and at the same time want it to end at the drop of a hat, it is most certainly possible and happens to all of us. In my poem *Follow My Lead* I am in a conversation with a woman that I am interested in. My interest in her is brand new and I have no idea what exactly what I want from her nor do I know when I want it, but I know that it's her that I want. My anxiety-urgency contradiction is shown in the following excerpt:

With you baby
I want you forever but I'm satisfied with tonight
You need to choose baby
If you want me too then for the rest of my natural life
I will pursue baby
If you give me a piece
You know that I'll want some more
No one else will have to know if I can get you all alone
On eternity's dance floor

I remember the exact situation that inspired this poem. I was at an after hours dance night for Argentine Tango dancers (a Milonga) and everyone there that night showed up to dance. Close embraces, beautiful moves, hearty laughs and the passion for dance filled the room. As a rookie dancer, I was beyond intimidated until a young lady on the opposite side of the room gave me the Tango cabeceo. (Side note: the cabeceo is subtle eye contact and a head nod to someone you are interested in dancing with and traditionally, men send the invitation to dance). I accepted her invitation and met her in the center of the dance circle. We danced for a few songs and I walked with her to her seat where we shared a magical conversation for a few short minutes before the night ended.

Lyrically, I captured the feelings dancing around in my head while we spoke which address how much I wanted to make that moment last and at the same time I knew I needed to state my case and get out before I mess something up. *"I want you forever but I'm satisfied with tonight,"* represents how wild my imagination ran with her in my future while also telling how great of a time my few minutes with her truly were. *"If you want me too then for the rest of my natural life I will pursue,"* represents how much I wanted to keep talking to her but my fear of failing to make a good impression made me unwilling to risk ending the conversation. These feelings happen to everyone every so often. Some thoughts I use to eliminate those feelings of uncertainty are used to remain in touch with my romantic intentions and never lose sight of my self worth.

The object of our affection obviously has something that we want. Acknowledging that desire is when we start to form our intentions and when talking about romantic intentions, flirting is a natural attention getter we all use to get those intentions met. Flirtation is a huge ego booster and the completion of a flirtatious encounter can turn a horrible day into a field of gumdrops and rainbows, but not all flirtation is with the intention of completing a romantic conquest. Flirting can also be used as a way to express appreciation, obtain goods or services with less effort or simply respond to someone flirting with you. This means that we must first know what our intentions are.

Somebody not in tune with their romantic intentions is liable to jump into a bad relationship or leave a potentially good relationship because they never had a grasp of what they wanted. Somebody not in tune with their self worth is likely to fall victim to an interesting conversation with someone that is completely wrong for them simply because the air of acceptance felt good at the time. The people deserted in a "hit it and quit it" situation are those that were not made aware of the deserter's intentions. This situation is different. No one can predict what someone else honestly wants from us and this uncertainty brings me back to knowing one's self worth.

Many people that are hurt by getting used and thrown away tend to blame themselves for not being good enough even though they know how amazing of a person they are. Never get caught in this trap. Always remember how valuable you are as a person so that even if you fall victim to someone with different intentions than you, your self worth can never come into question. Along with knowing your self worth we must also keep in mind that the urgency to hold on to the first conversation we discussed earlier can come from deprivation, which may lead to acts of desperation and poor decision making.

My poem *More Than Sex* was written after a whirlwind weekend fling with a girl from college that I had pursued to no avail for over two years. One day during a sexless period lasting over six months, she and I were coincidentally forced to work together on a class project. Completely ignoring the assignment, the events described in the poem transpired over the course of that weekend. Out of touch with my own romantic intentions and feeling so unwanted, I fell victim to a hit it and quit it deserter and was subject to months of awkward emotional confusion simply because I was desperate and didn't even realize.

Understand that at this point for me, I was not just desperate for sex or attention; I was desperate for validation. It was easy for her to get her intentions fulfilled because hers were clear. Had I been in tune with what I was looking for and confident enough to make her aware of my expectations, I would not have accidentally fulfilled her intentions. Instead, I would have either been fully aware that I was engaging in sexual anonymity or I simply would not have engaged her in the first place if my wants didn't match hers. Understand that we develop and pursue intentions within relationships as well.

The different types of intentions within a relationship come from a variety of reasons to be together ranging from the traditional (sex, marriage, money, etc.) to the distinctive (abusive control, attachment, arrangement, citizenship, etc.). From those of us in a brand new relationship to those of us that have been together for years, everyone has intentions for themselves and their partner and it is perfectly normal for those intentions to shift, change or evolve… so long as that person stays in touch with their intentions and shares it with their significant other.

I believe that the most common intention shift is the scenario whereby the original agreement of the relationship is not to get emotionally involved, but one or both participants develop feelings outside of the agreement. Another commonly changing intention is the desire for marriage or the desire to have children. Sometimes we enter relationships with no intention of an event like marriage, children or even love itself, but our human needs change as we grow and evolve.

Always remain in touch with yourself and what you want for your life because it is the only way that you can truly experience joy. To not pursue what it is that you want out of life is to cage yourself in a prison of misery because you will feel as though you are wasting your life every single day.

The same concept applies with suppressing your intentions for a relationship and keeping your feelings hidden. Are we afraid to reveal a new intention because we don't want to scare away our partner with this new version of us or are we afraid because we actually fear the possibility of getting exactly what we want and are afraid of messing it up? See **Exercise 2** in the appendix to put your intentions in front of your own face.

It can be very difficult to see our own reality without an outside perspective. Short of friends and family telling us what we "need to hear", it can definitely help to see a different perspective when you put yourself onto paper or hear yourself talk aloud. Think about this exercise like those times where an idea sounds great in your head, but when you say it out loud, you realize that it's completely not. You will be able to hear what you want and what you have experienced out loud. From there you can decide if your intentions match what you have dealt with, what you are dealing with or what you are willing to deal with.

Although there is no way to tell the future, anyone can learn from the past.

   After bragging to your friends about how incredible and fantastic this person was that you met and neurotically stressing that you weren't funny or interesting enough, you get out of the shower three nights after our hypothetical encounter to see a missed phone call and voicemail from the object of your affection. You are requested for dinner and a movie this Friday and your hilariously empty schedule sends chills through your body. You look in the mirror and look into your eyes with your game face on. It's time to put your money where your mouth is. It's time to put up or shut up. It's time to show them what you're made of. It's time to let him or her know that you are interested and not seem desperate while making sure they know how amazing you are on the inside without seeming like you're cocky but still show them your personality avoiding embarrassing faults about yourself during your display of how much fun you can be yet not do anything that you couldn't live up to. Sound confusing? That's because it absolutely is.

3

Pursuit

The handshake of every relationship in the history of mankind has finally arrived; the first date. You put on your most flattering and fashionable outfit, spray on your most tantalizing scent, turn off the lights in your spotlessly cleaned residence and meet up with someone that sends your senses into overload. During your conversation, it seems like every question asked makes you feel closer and more familiar because more and more information is getting shared outdoing the feeling of the first time you spoke. Something is different in the way you speak though.

It's almost as though you're choosing to tell a very selective truth about yourself. All responses about yourself are bigger and sound grander than if you were to be telling the same story to a friend. Every tale about your life, work and hobbies is a tale of valor, success and grandeur; maybe even your job title gets a few syllables longer. How is it that the story of you spilling coffee all over your boss on the morning of your promotion got left out of the story behind you getting promoted?

Take any other detail we purposefully neglect to mention. Are we secretly embarrassed about ourselves and wish not to share the entirety of our being so that we don't seem uncool or is it that we have developed a system where embarrassing truth, no matter how small, is supposed to be left out until further into knowing someone new? It seems to me that we have developed this "honesty filter" from our socially advanced version of the primitive mating dance done in the animal kingdom.

From the most beautiful train of the peacock, to the biggest horns on a goat or sheep, down to the strongest stench of the ring-tailed lemur, the rituals of attracting a mate are not so different between human beings and the rest of the animal kingdom; the most grand display of strength, wealth and sexual prowess. Humans differ in the grandeur of these displays but there is at least one animal out there that does one of the things that we do to attract a mate. The bowerbird builds a very difficult and beautiful shrine called a "bower" to attract the attention of a willing female. The African elephant spends anywhere from one hour to several days courting one another before copulation. Heck, even the red-capped manakin does the Moonwalk to attract his mate (trust me, you have to YouTube it because it's awesome).

The best foot gets put forward and all of these animals' strengths are displayed to get some attention or they will not be able to pass on their genes. On the other side of this coin, if an animal is having problems with its health, hygiene or hospitality, it would be best for them to conceal their faults until after their display is accepted and a mate chooses them. Sound familiar?

Our ritual starts off with conversation by being the most interesting, funny, witty and intelligent person we can be to attract the attention of a willing mate. Just like in the animal kingdom, our first line of attraction is to be the perfect candidate and that usually means we are going to try and do our best to avoid the part of our story that is humiliating or unflattering so that our display is as flawless as possible. The irony about this practice is that most people are truthfully not looking for the perfect person to be with. Deep down, most of us know that we ourselves are not perfect.

See **Exercise 3** in the appendix and answer some questions about the way that you once viewed these extremely embarrassing events when they happened compared to the way you see them now. We can try to hide it all we want to but our quirky, clumsy and weird side is adorable when we are comfortable with it. We could have it way worse. The water strider is a bug that taps its leg against the surface of the water to attract fish in order to rush the female to want to mate faster before being eaten, porcupines urinate on their potential partner and white-front parrots vomit in each other's mouths.

Even though these things have probably happened somewhere in the world on the first date (trust me when I literally say 'shit happens'), we also have to realize that there is an approachable quality in being perfectly imperfect. Not saying that you need to be so honest that you release an earth-rumbling fart or freely chew louder than a Neanderthal, but on average none of us want to feel as though the person we want to be with has no faults. There is a natural insecurity complex that we have toward mates that seem far superior to us which is why we have these notions of someone being "too good for you" or "out of your league".

No one is too good for anyone else. Often times, the material things someone has the most of are shown off far more often so that they can hide their insecurities. If she has more money than you, it's very possible that she doesn't get her funny bone tickled very often since she is likely wrapped up in serious business more than socially interacting so be sure to make her laugh. If he exists in a higher level of popularity or celebrity, treat him like a normal person with normal thoughts and feelings because it's likely that his fans, supporters and investors rarely treat him as anything less than an icon. Being yourself is about as bold as you can get these days and if you want to make a bold statement, you know exactly what to do to get them to recognize you. We've talked about being the pursuer, but what about the position of being the pursued?

To be pursued into love is an interesting position to be in because even as a man, I've had the privilege of being pursued in the way that human males are traditionally expected to pursue. Understanding both sides of the fence in this way, I've noticed that pushiness and desperation know no gender in the mating dance. One of my least favorite things about the pursuit phase is the idea of playing hard to get. I feel like it's one of the masks that we place on ourselves to make the world believe that we're something we're not.

Understand that playing hard to get does not only apply to the refusal of sexual favors but also to pretending to be more cynical and finicky than usual or asking for and expecting more than necessary as some sort of test to make sure the pursuer is truly interested. I don't know the statistics but I can only hope that these childish tactics don't work on the vast majority of humans. If someone knows themselves enough to know that they truly *are* hard to get, then by all means they have their right to be themselves, but in no way should anyone *play* hard to get. Then they're just showing ugly feathers covered in berry juices like a deformed peacock or angering another Silverback gorilla and claiming the loudness from the resulting aggression as their own.

It's quite simply a lie that won't result in an honest interaction between those two people. Even certain rules that we tend to follow to *not* seem desperate or clingy come from insecurity and fear. The ever-so high school "3-day rule" for calling someone you've met is so strange to me. I slipped it into the beginning of this chapter and you have to ask yourself why it has to take so long. Contact information was exchanged in order for the two of you to contact one another. A nurse might be extremely busy during the week so it might not be the most practical idea to call six times a day, leaving four voicemails and a text message every hour on the hour. A yoga instructor may have a free block of time between morning and evening classes for a social life so it may not be the most practical idea to ignore his or her card for a month and try to force yourself into their life at your leisure.

Of course there are limits into how soon and how often to reach out to make contact, but when you think about it, that limit changes from person to person so following a definitive rule is not a realistic solution. When being pursued, act natural and everything will work itself out, whether the interaction should continue or not.

The hypothetical date went by without a hitch. You were witty, funny and more relaxed than you have been in a long while but you were also attentive and receptive to what your date had to say. It has finally come to a sorrowful conclusion but you feel more accomplished now that they have a sense of the real you including your weird laugh, your spoon on the nose trick and the story of stubbing your sixth toe. You extend your hand for a thank you handshake or outstretch your arms for a goodnight hug and WHAM... your dream plants a full-blown Disney wedding kiss you. I don't know how you folks out there in love land view wins-and-losses, but this is a win in my book; and this is my book. BOOM! So you got what you've been thinking about for the last three and a half blissful hours. What now?

4

Conquest

The most enjoyable evening in your life has come to a close and the most enjoyable night of your life is potentially about to start. Eyes glaring deeply into one another's, fingers intertwining in a nervously clammy grip, arms wrapping around necks, waists and backs or lips locking in the adoring embrace of a passionate kiss, the time you two have spent together is resonating between you with no sign of slowing down. At this point, the evening has touched you in a way that you feel naturally connected to one another and every bone in your body is telling you to live for the moment and let what happens unfold naturally. Sadly, this is also the point that you have been conditioned by our society to begin to scrutinize your feelings, desires and intentions because you wouldn't want to make yourself seem too easy, attainable or desperate. Would you?

When I spoke earlier about being and feeling desperate or easy, those instances were all about avoiding those feelings *about* you coming *from* yourself. Now we are getting into the psychology of trying to keep other people from viewing you in this light. In order to do this, we first have to examine how people perceive one another based on their conditioning.

Everyone in modern society has his or her way of thinking and operating when it comes to romantic connections. Demisexual people are not initially attracted physically to their partner but later develop sexual feelings once they are deeply emotionally involved. Pansexual people can be literally attracted to all kinds of people with absolutely no regard for gender bias. Sapiosexual people develop sexual arousal from the enjoyment of another person's intelligence and can experience the same chemical reactions that occur during sexual pleasure from intellectual conversation.

No matter what a person's sexual orientation, I feel that everyone in our society is impacted in some way by the influence of television, movies, theater and music. I developed a theory about the courting practices of men and women of my generation that we court each other like action heroes and Disney princesses. (Follow me on this one).

For decades, Walt Disney has been making movies about princesses in situations that they needed to be rescued from. Jasmine was bored, Belle was broke, Ariel was horny, Rapunzel was lonely, Snow White was dead and the list goes on. The dilemmas that they found themselves facing were all thwarted by the heroic and valiant efforts of a man that comes to save the day. Prince Charming, Prince

Eric, Aladdin, The Beast and Prince Naveen all seem to appear out of nowhere in the story and through masterful storytelling save their damsels in distress. The underlying message, though, conditions little girls to believe that a perfectly chiseled knight in shining armor or draped in the finest of clothes is going to swoop in and save her from her problems because she needs *a* man (the italicized *a* sounds like 'ay' and basically means "any").

Conversely, action heroes have valiantly graced the big screen in blockbuster films and proved their masculinity by saving the world time and time again. James Bond, Rambo, The Transporter, Shaft and John McClane barely scroll down the list of ripped martial arts fighting, big gun blasting heroes that save the world and get the girl in the first film and do it all over again with another girl in the sequel. Little boys are not conditioned to be *a* man, but instead to be *the* man (the italicized *the* sounds like 'thee' and basically means "the greatest and only"). An issue arises when a conditioned Disney princess looking for her knight in shining armor winds up finding herself in the arms of a conditioned action hero.

She is looking for *a* (any) man to make her happy but she comes across the man that believes himself to be *the* (the greatest and only) man. In this scenario, she is undoubtedly going to get replaced after he completes his mission and moves on to the theoretical sequel. The way for us to recondition ourselves is to teach our little boys what it means to be *a* man and to teach our little girls that their power lies within with additional room for someone else to join them in their self-sufficiency.

Even keeping with the fantasy analogy here, I see a mix up in what roles should be played. Women look for a knight in shining armor and men try to be that knight when in reality, the goal should be to be, and tame, the dragon. The knight does only what is in his own interest and hides his true self behind the illusion of a beautiful shell like the shiny cars of the action movies. Here, the dragon represents a man striving to become unafraid to be his real self with no other interest but to protect his princess. Instead of waiting for a knight to rescue her, these "trapped" princesses must learn to tame the dragon itself realizing that she is actually being protected. Here, the dragon represents a woman's virtue to herself first and foremost thwarting the careless and thoughtless efforts of unworthy suitors. Popular culture conditioning aside, we still need to discuss some ideas how to overcome society's rules about how to deal with our feelings at this point in the evening; the night cap.

The point in our date, or outing, where there is no curfew or foreseeable conclusion is the point where the night either concludes exactly as planned or ends up in complete disaster. Magical fairy tale endings happen when both participants have the same ending goal in mind. Depending on who you are and what you want from the remainder of the evening, your expectations will sometimes differ from the person you are out with.

From a simple handshake and kiss on the cheek all the way down to rug burns and bodily fluids everywhere, different evenings end differently either to be enjoyed for the moment at hand or to be repeated continuously (i.e. one time encounter, finite occurrences or permanent recurrence). Divulging those expectations is the tricky part because not only are we brought up to be apprehensive to reveal our innermost desires toward other people, the power of the double standard keeps us scared to be ourselves.

A double standard is a rule or principle that is unfairly applied to different people or groups. The double standard applied in this phase of our relationship scenario is that even if both of you are experiencing natural feelings of attraction and attachment toward one another, you are not supposed to explore them to avoid a reputation ruining stigma. Even though no one seems to understand or agree with these unwritten rules, there are those of us that genuinely have a personal respect for the sanctity of marriage and the treatment of the body as a temple. I tip my hat to them. To abstain from sexually charged encounters is an admirable and spiritually cleansing practice. However, often times the rest of us simply do not honestly state our intentions because we don't want to get labeled as a dog (men) or a whore (women).

I think that the romantic double standard is not only unfair; it is also largely untrue. Preconceived notions about gender roles and responsibilities only apply some of the time and not necessarily to the gender they are applied to. A man that is accustomed to being an exploratory bachelor sometimes has the urge to take things slowly and avoid the complications of an early sexual encounter with someone he is interested in. A woman that is normally accustomed to a sex life only with partners to whom she is monogamously committed is well within her rights to indulge herself in the fruits of her own desires for companionship. My theory as to why these roles are so set is due to our biological responsibility to reproduce.

If a man wants to court a woman in an ideal world, he will bring her flowers, take her out on dates, share a first kiss, fall in love, get married, have sex and have babies. If we were to go back 500 years to 16th century European courtship practices, a man and a woman would either inherit wealth or property or amass needed wealth to be able to afford economic independence within the union, they would publicly ritualize their union in front of their peers, have sex and have babies. Take it back 10,000 years to the hunter-gatherer societies of the modern human and our chemical attractions to each other bring us together simply to have sex and have babies. In the primitive sense, a pregnant woman is linked to her man for the next nine months while her man is only linked to her until he desires to spread his seed again and again with other women. This is why I believe the stereotypes of men being inherently polygamous and women being inescapably attachable exist but we also do not live in prehistoric times anymore.

As much as our society tries to make us feel wrong for our urges to enjoy our natural sexuality, I believe that we should all be comfortable enough to explore our sexual reality so that there can be no miscommunications in our desires for one another. We are already given an endless list of rules about things like: what to eat, where to live, what to drive, how to smell, what to buy, when to shave, what to watch and how to act like an adult. I couldn't imagine that we as humans will ever fully accept rules on who and how to love. Our mass media is notorious for demonizing certain groups of people while glorifying other groups and through it all, there are always examples of couples that fight through what their environment tells them is wrong and unacceptable because they are sure of themselves.

Our instincts and feelings matter and it is high time that we stand up for what we want in our lives that no one else will live to the fullest but us. See **Exercise 4** in the appendix to chart how far things went with your romantic partners and ask yourself why they went there, why they stopped or why they happened at all. Many times feelings of guilt, remorse, shame and regret accompany our sexual histories and those feelings mostly arise after the deed has been done. If this is the case, then we must shed the stereotypical notions that we've been labeled with for so long and take our sex lives back. Man or woman, you are within your right as a human being to explore your feelings no matter what it is that you want to do or how long you want to take to do it.

The sun rises on the two of you and sends your Cinderella fairy tale evening dashing out of the castle before the proverbial stroke of midnight. Each person reading this has a different idea of what has happened throughout an entire night with his or her significant other. Some readers envisioned themselves talking on the phone about everything imaginable from the excitement of the evening to stories from his or her childhood. Some readers saw themselves cuddling together near a flickering fireplace or wrapped together in a blanket on the beach. Some readers foresee themselves unlocking their partner from the consensually applied fuzzy handcuffs, cleaning up the pieces from the broken lamp and patching up the headboard that inflicted damage to the bedroom wall after removing jumper cables from the nipple clamps on his or her full body latex suit coarse from candlewax residue.

Whatever your desired outcome, you and your companion agreed on one thing; tonight would happen naturally and everything would be perfect. Contrary to what has happened in your love life before this, everything did turn out perfectly and you agree to see one another again. The second date turns into a third date and so on, but something you didn't expect is happening. No matter what you do, you can't think about anything in life without it reminding you of them. You both want to be together more and more as time goes on almost as though you couldn't control your feelings for one another. Well… that's because you can't control it. We call it *falling* in love for a reason.

Phase 2

Love

5

Captivation

Walking hand in hand along a beautiful sun kissed beach, gazing into each other's eyes in a late night malt shop sharing a delicious milkshake and laughing hysterically while huddled together in a chilly movie theater might only be the first of many activities you and your newfound love share with one another. Now that you both agree on the goals for your relationship, you can finally release the pressure you've placed on yourself to do everything right in their eyes. Now you can enjoy your time together and allow your inhibitions to fall away.

This is the most interesting and exciting time of any relationship. Every piece of information is a new and exciting surprise ranging from where your partner grew up, where they went to school, what jobs they've worked in the past, when they learned how to cook, what their relationship with their family was like, etc. Every moment you share together is thought about throughout the day making simple tasks like paying attention at work or school, driving, cleaning or shopping almost impossible without your object of affection coming to mind.

Deeply rooted emotional involvement has officially begun for the both of you and you know that you can see yourself with this person for the rest of your life. However, in these inaugural months of your relationship you must take care that you keep your expectations in mind because without thinking you can fall for someone that stands for nothing.

The beginning of any romantic journey should make you feel nervous, excited, anxious, joyful, scared, courageous and free and it's likely that you can experience all of these feelings changing from one to another in a very short time. This period is referred to as puppy love because of how quickly and easily puppies tend to devote themselves to their owners, but I like to think of the name with a different approach.

Puppies have a lack of awareness of their surroundings due to how excitable they are about everything new, enchanting and unfamiliar around them. Puppies get accidentally stepped on, almost sat on, nearly run over by vehicles and dognapped every single day, not to any fault of their own, because they are so fascinated by this new world they want to play in that they don't notice some very obvious dangers. If these dangers could be avoided, their play time could be more aware, safer and in many cases more fun.

We must think of ourselves as a puppy owner. The

puppy is our heart and the things to play with in the world (let's say a dog park) are the personal attributes of our romantic interest. This puppy of ours wants nothing more than to play with all the new and exciting toys, run around in the fresh grass and interact with the other puppies, but without caution because since everything is so new and exciting it's difficult for them to think cautiously. When beginning a relationship it is very easy to allow our hearts to frolic in this fashion without regard for pitfalls in the other person's personality that may not match the preferences we've already set for ourselves (refer to Chapter 2 discussing intentions and preferences). This "puppy" love rarely results in long standing relationships and falling for it is as easy as ABC; Attributes Before Characteristics.

It is very easy for someone to put their best foot forward when it comes to impressing the one they are romantically interested in. It is far more difficult to receive the display of that best foot without confusing what their romantic interest has and what they do with who their romantic interest is as a person. A person's attributes include things such as: occupation, physical appearance, learned abilities, financial status, collection of personal belongings and personal experiences. Although there is an endless list of each of the before mentioned attributes (i.e. multi-millionaire, massage therapist, visited Rome, ran a marathon, collects unicorn stamps, built like Beyoncé, etc.) these things could never determine a person's character.

Anyone can get any job. Anyone can have great genes. Anyone can take a class to learn how to do anything in the world. None of these attributes matter if their personal characteristics are not desired. A person's characteristics are states of being such as: caring, giving, selfish, rude, outgoing, cynical, lazy, funny, compassionate and honest. There are far more characteristics to list, but the difference is that characteristics are much harder to change and impossible to hide for very long. See **Exercise 5** in the appendix to take a look into your personal characteristics that make you who you are. In order for a relationship to thrive, you have to understand the person you are and then become the person you would want to be with.

Imagine a high school principal that is polite and compassionate yet proactive going out to dinner with an engineer who is condescending and irritable yet lazy. Let's say their server had only been with the restaurant for two days. As the evening progresses, the server may forget to check on the table, refill a drink or put in an incorrect order but he or she is genuinely apologetic, thoroughly engaged in fulfilling the table's needs and strongly accommodating for his or her mistakes. Snide remarks, an impatient demeanor and a cynical attitude coming from the engineer will likely turn off the principal. Submissive understanding, complacent optimism and incompetence allowance will likely turn off the engineer.

Regardless of their shared interest in reading Dan Brown conspiracy thriller novels, rebuilding and restoring classic cars, participating in water sports or investing in the stock market, they would never be able to sustain a long-term relationship because their beliefs and personalities differ in ways that do not work together harmoniously. Often times we trick ourselves into allowing these types of differences-better known as red flags- to exist in the beginning parts of our relationships because we don't want to offend our new interest by telling them that their behavior is not desired or appreciated. I personally think that this honesty is exactly what society has been missing for quite some time. If we were to be that honest more often, we would either influence the undesired behavior to change or free ourselves from a potentially damaging relationship to remain available for someone more suited to our desires in a partner.

We should start to make the most important things about a person we're interested in the things can can't be destroyed by fire. From my early years of high school I began to observe the materialistic and impressionable reasons that many relationships stem from. I told myself that if an aspect of my life can be destroyed in a fire, it is not important to attract a woman. My looks, my car, my place of residence, my clothes, my bank account, or anything else of surface value can be taken away from me in an instant by the searing flames of a blazing inferno. This is why I prefer to concentrate on developing a winning personality.

To become more genuine, honest, patient, kind, caring,

giving, compassionate, sensitive, proactive, determined and ambitious is to become a person that places importance in things that cannot be taken away in mere moments. In the following excerpt from my poem *Smile* I am speaking about myself during a time where I lost sight of the open and honest man that I want to continue to become and it took the understanding and patience of a young lady I was seeing to get me back on track.

Most men are so used to running from their feelings
We just need someone to listen sometimes
Only a lover can bring us to that healing
How about you sit him down and give it a try
When a woman tries to judge a man
About something she doesn't understand
She brings a pain that can build into rage and animosity
Say something she doesn't mean and then nobody is happy
Make him smile for you
Tell him you love it when he smiles for you
We act like it's not really our style to do
You already have so much to prove
If you can show him how
He will smile for you and bring a wedding and a child to you
First you have to ease his hurtin and make certain
He smiles for you

I was less than proud of certain aspects of my past and when she would ask me questions about how I turned out to be who I am, I shut her out with anger and frustration. However, it was her understanding and patience with me that helped me to ease back into my promise to myself to be honest and understanding even toward my own faults.

Although that relationship didn't last, it was an experience that carried me forward to be a better person in future relationships. I believe that as long as we are honest about what we are willing to associate ourselves with and learn lessons from the events of our past, it is going to get easier for people to find their perfect romantic match.

At this point you and your sweetheart have given your time to one another for several months. You have become very comfortable around each other and he or she has proven themself to be everything you have ever wanted in a partner. On one of your typical nights basking in the magical glow of his or her awesomeness, your darling breaks the silence of a long pause after a fit of hysterical laughter with all of the words you want to hear. "I really like you", "this time with you has been everything I've ever dreamed of" and "when I'm with you I really feel like I can be myself" are but a few of the sweet nothings causing your heart to melt and your knees to buckle.

If you're like many people that have been cynically ruined by romantic comedies, these phrases might bring a level of uneasiness and an impending doom that they will be followed by a mood killing "but", but they aren't. The conversation actually heads in a direction that you were waiting to bring up yourself; a conversation that you've been waiting your whole life to have with someone like this; a conversation about taking your personal status as a single person and changing it. You've been asked to become part of a world where every aspect of life is liable to be shared, decisions are no longer needed to be made alone and emotions reign supreme. You have just been asked to date exclusively.

6

Fulfillment

Every bad date, weird compliment, misjudged character, bonehead mistake and lonely night have all led to this very moment. Your sweaty palms, cotton mouth and thundering heartbeat all make it fairly difficult to fully grasp the gravity of being asked to enter into an exclusive relationship with the love of your life, but it happened. Actually, it's still happening. "You've been thinking about this very moment for months now; open your mouth and say YES, already!" you tell yourself in your mind but only able to utter a tiny squeak in reality. You eventually say yes while the love of your life smiles with adoration at the best thing that has ever happened to them; you.

In these scenarios we glorify our feelings toward the object of our collective affection, but in reality it takes both parties involved to feel the same in order for true love to shine through the darkness of our pessimistic society. Some readers may have latched onto my usage of the term "true love" with a raised eyebrow because of my views on the Disney paradigm and that confusion is justified. Let me go on record to say that I firmly do not believe in true love, in the way that "true love" is described. Love is beautiful, enchanting and exciting but it can also be confusing, difficult and sometimes discouraging and although I believe in the power of love, I completely disagree with the idea of an effortless happily ever after.

The ending of all fairy tales finishes with most of the happy couples living happily ever after. At some point we all find ourselves watching the big movie kiss and hearing the wedding bells ringing thinking of how much we want real life to be like in the stories. If we can get past our juvenile expectations of how a relationship is supposed to go we would all realize that not only is the storybook ending impossible, it makes absolutely no sense.

For example, Prince Eric from "The Little Mermaid" fell in love with Ariel and she didn't even talk to him. How many people have you ever fallen in love with that didn't say a word? I always thought that silence was supposed to be awkward. The Prince from "Snow White and the Seven Dwarfs" was walking through the woods, found Snow White lying in her coffin and woke her up with a kiss. How many people have ever been in love with a necrophiliac? If she bites him he's going to turn into a zombie. Prince Charming in "Cinderella" searched the countryside for the woman that fit the glass slipper left behind by his true bride. How many people have ever fallen in love with someone who didn't even know what you looked like? I mean, what would have happened if another thin blonde chick in the kingdom wore a size 7?

These relationships would not hold any merit in the real world because the plot lines leading up to them living happily ever after would never happen. Even if they really did happen, there is no way that those couples lived the rest of their lives together without an argument, disagreement or misunderstanding. This brings me to my main point about true love being false in the way we've been taught because we were given the wrong definition of love. I will explain my theory in greater detail later on in the book, but first I don't want to forget that you are fresh into an exclusive relationship! We haven't even talked about what that can mean for you two lovebirds.

New relationships are formed all the time because there are many people in the world searching to be a part of something greater than them. For this new relationship to flourish, you must first come to an understanding of likes, dislikes, tolerances, pet peeves and preferences. A big mistake for new relationships is that these discussions rarely happen until after a problem has already developed. Two people combining their lives after years of living, doing things and behaving a certain way is obviously going to bring about clashes and disagreements. The biggest clash that isn't typically discussed until it's too late is how to differentiate friendliness from flirtation from infidelity.

As we have discussed previously (see chapter 2), everyone should have a strong sense of what they want out of a relationship. If your rules for fidelity are not a part of the list, they definitely need to be added. If you don't know what you think cheating is, then you are either expecting them to "get it" or you're leaving them to figure it out on their own; neither of which are effective for long-lasting relationships.

Everyone is different in what we think cheating is and isn't. Some believe that simply looking at another person is a form of cheating while others feel that as long as all clothes stay on and there is no contact with genitalia then it's not cheating. There are some relationships that operate in the way that Kanye West describes: "We've formed a new religion. No sins as long as there's permission and deception is the only felony so never fuck nobody without telling me." This brand of open relationship is free to roam sexually and to cheat is to not disclose a sex act while swingers, another form of an open relationship, believe that contacting an extramarital lover outside the swinging act is considered cheating.

Even though we are all very different, it is important to tell your partner how you feel so that what is acceptable and what is unacceptable becomes common knowledge. There are many other conversations that we should have in the beginning of a new relationship, but now that we've gotten the big one out of the way it's time to talk about your new life together.

Joining lives with another person is an interesting and beneficial process. Both people discover new places to eat and shop, improved methods of cooking and cleaning and a consistent companion to comfort and entertain them just by sharing with each other. There is one area of your worlds coming together that sometimes causes problems and that area is the circle of friends that is now involved in your union.

Friends and family have been proven to be very therapeutic for relationships when issues arise and an outside view is needed to figure out a course of action. In this comfort, we sometimes neglect to include our significant other in the conversation. Here, a situation arises where the friends know more about the problems within the relationship more than the significant other that is causing the problem in the first place.

Even if you need outside help or advice, I think it is crucial to always be up front and honest with your partner whenever a potential problem arises. Most of the time we tell the story of an argument or a misunderstanding from our own perspective and do not admit to our contributions to the problems and this creates a one-sided imbalance of opinion within the friendship circle.

If a boyfriend always tell his friends about how much his girlfriend nags him about picking up his shoes, his friends will likely be under the impression that she is an incessant nag. This boyfriend would most likely never tell his friends that she discussed the cleanliness of the household several times with a calm and understanding tone and he simply never respected her wishes. This is only one example of using a friendship circle to help council us through our relationship issues and how it can be a detriment to finding a practical solution to the problem itself.

If the above mentioned boyfriend would ask his girlfriend why she treats him the way she does, she then has the opportunity to remind him of how may times she made the original request. With this open and honest conversation, they can hopefully come to a clear conclusion to the issue without friends and family simply bad mouthing the partner that can't defend his or herself. We do not want to focus on arguments though! How about we change gears and talk about how completely devoted you two are going to be to one another and the process that comes along with it? Is that a yes? AWESOME!

Unless you are a teenager or very reserved, if you've made it to this part of a romantic interaction you have had other people that you were once romantically interested in. If that is the case then you probably know that as soon as you tell the world that you are in a new relationship, everyone from your past seems to want to contact you all of a sudden. That ex-girlfriend that messed up really bad or the one guy you spent spring break with a few years back will start texting, messaging or calling again. Even in the regular world it seems like when we enter into an exclusive relationship, everyone walking down the street all of a sudden gets more attractive and more interested in you. I want to shed some light on this phenomenon.

In my opinion, it's simply our natural human complex to

want things we can't have. The complex especially takes hold when there is something we once had that someone else has now. This idea goes back to infanthood. A baby that wants a toy he or she is being denied will just want that toy more and more. Even if you give the toy to the baby and start playing with a toy he or she was no longer playing with, the baby will then want the toy you have. The same rules apply to the territorial ways that humans claim one another.

Past lovers, flames and interests have a tendency to have a sort of "seller's remorse" toward your affection when you decide give it to someone else. They usually approach when there is some type of issue in their own love life and they want to feel the flames of your old fire because it's obvious that yours is burning bright. DO NOT FALL FOR IT!!! If you are truly committed to the person you are now with, you will neither allow nor entertain the thought of backstepping into an old relationship.

I think that with strangers, we begin to exude a certain level of confidence and sexuality when we are happily involved and other people can sense it. There is something extremely appealing about a person that other people want and the random hot dude or cute chick passing you in the mall can sense that somebody wants you bad. That's why they bat their eye or flash a smirk. DO NOT FALL FOR IT!!! In your mind you might feel the flattery and think it means you deserve to be a little adventurous, but please remember that your partner is the reason you had that extra pep in your step to feel that way in the first place. See **Exercise 6** in the appendix and find out what exactly you are focused on in this new relationship. You may gain some insight into the way that you perceive relationships right now.

Okay now, come on. You guys need to get a room everywhere you go. You've gotten rid of your little black books, added up all of the kisses and hugs you gave to everyone you've ever dated, multiplied that number times infinity and given that much love to your partner. You now have families and friends deeply involved in your union and your relationship is blossoming beautifully. Everything is going according to plan until one night over the phone.

Your partner tells you that he or she has loved spending time with you, you are a really wonderful person and follows these amazing compliments with, "This is hard for me to say." The cliché DJ scratch sound goes off in your mind when you hear that last part. In no universe do those words ever lead to something good. Right? Well then stop thinking and pay attention! "This is hard for me to say… because I've never said this and meant it. I love you. I am *in* love with you." Sooooo… ummmmm… uh oh. Your heart is about to stop beating isn't it? Don't die yet, you haven't said it back yet. Well… go ahead!

7

Attachment

"Well, say something would you?" your partner pleas. It has literally been thirty seconds of dead silence on the phone while tears stream down your face from joy. You run a full blown photo montage through your mind of all the good times you shared during the previous several months leading up to this moment; the big moment when one of you drops the L-bomb. You lovingly reply in the only way you should really respond to someone you genuinely love. "I love you too!"

FINALLY!!! It's out there. You two are in love. You thought that this would happen the day he or she walked up to you at that bar or in that park or outside that grocery store, but I want to make sure that you two get the credit that you deserve. I'm going to change my phrase from "you two are in love" to "you two love one another". I don't want to tell you that you are "in love" because I don't believe in being "in love"; not in the sense that we're taught anyway. We are taught that two people that love one another are considered to have fallen in love, but if you look back at all of the time you spent together and all of the energy you put into being with one another you would never use a word like "falling" to describe that process. Your love was purposeful and intentional right? Well then, I want to bring you to my grand idea that we have been taught wrong what the definition of love really is.

I charge you to look up the definition of the word love. The closest definition I found came from the Merriam-Webster Collegiate Dictionary 11th Edition and it reads, "unselfish loyal and benevolent concern for the good of another." I agree with the way that love is described here, but it lacks the fundamental nature of being an action verb. Take the phrase *I love* you and say it out loud thinking of the word love as an action. To love means that you show the actions necessary for someone to see that you have an unselfish, loyal and benevolent concern for them, but that is not all that love is.

Love is changing the way you think about something that once irritated you to your wits end in order to accommodate the person you *love*. Love is telling the complete and honest truth about the person you *love* even if it may be difficult to hear or receive. The best explanation of love comes from the New International Version of the Bible in 1 Corinthians 13: 4-8. It reads, "4 Love is patient, love is kind. It does not envy, it does not boast, it is not proud. 5 It does not dishonor others, it is not self-seeking, it is not easily angered, it keeps no record of wrongs. 6 Love does not delight in evil but rejoices with the truth.

7 It always protects, always trusts, always hopes, always perseveres. 8 Love never fails." Even here, *love* as a noun should be transformed to an action verb *to love*. To love is to show patience. To love is to be kind. These are actions people that love one another show in order to show their partner how much they are *loved*. Let's go even further into how wrongly our usage of love is by going into the critical phrase "I love you".

This is the moment that your partner has finally told you that they love you. In some cases, this might be the moment where you are telling your partner that you love him or her. In either case, this is the first time that the powerful feeling of love has been discussed and without an almost immediate return the moment can get very awkward very fast. Many people hesitate to be the first one in a relationship to say "I love you" because they don't want to be the first to reveal the deepest part of their feelings. I have heard and interviewed many people saying that they hesitate to say it first because the first person to say it loses power in the relationship and it's awkward to wait for the "I love you too" response.

Firstly, if your relationship is based on who has the most power then you are either in an emotionally abuse relationship or you have the concept of an equal partnership completely messed up. Secondly, our new way of thinking about the way we use the word *love* means that there is no need for a return other than to satisfy our own ego that the person we love actually loves us in return. If I were to say that I love someone, based on what we talked about a few paragraphs ago, I am saying that I have feelings of adoration, honesty and loyalty toward that person.

In relationships where enough time has passed and one partner declares their love for the other partner, the feeling is probably mutual. However, that is not always the case (even though we obviously want the feeling to be mutual). It is possible to love someone that does not love you the same way because, remember, your love is based on the way that you feel and the energy that you are willing to put into the person you love. It has nothing to do with the way that the relationship has progressed thus far. When you hear "I love you too" it should not simply be a relief that you heard it back because the moment would have otherwise been awkward.

When you hear or say "I love you too" it should be a declaration that the feeling of being loyal to, interested in and smitten by the other partner is shared by you both. It's not just a reply so that nobody feels weird they said it first. Take it very seriously when you say it. We're going to go even deeper into the idea of love and discuss how to show someone that we love him or her.

In order to have a harmonious and long-lasting relationship, you and your partner need to study one another in order to figure out exactly how each of you perceives love. Everyone loves differently and everyone receives love differently so it is critical to be sensitive to the different ways that your partner gives and receives love. Gary Chapman wrote a book entitled *The Heart of the Five Love Languages* and this text separates the ways that we show love into five categories: words of affirmation, quality time, receiving gifts, acts of service and physical touch. Every one of us should be familiar with which of these acts we feel are more important than the others.

I dated a young lady that would absolutely refuse to hold my hand, kiss me in public or even cuddle after sex. Telling her how beautiful I found her and how deeply in love with her I was, she shrugged her shoulders with the bland thank you one could expect from a celebrity when an adoring fan swoons over their performance. However, one Valentine's Day I paid to get her nails done, bought her a teddy bear that read, "Te Amo," (she is half Mexican), paid for a big sushi dinner and took her out to the movies. I also gave her a very expensive Victoria's Secret bra that I got for free since I worked there, but was still a great gift. That night, the intimacy level flew through the roof. I felt as though it was a false sense of intimacy because I spent hundreds of dollars on our Valentine's Day celebration, so I decided to tell her that the bra was free. She... Lost... Her... MIND!!!

Everything else that had been done was completely voided because the bra was free and for years I simply thought that she was a materialistic woman, but in time I realized that the exchange of gifts is her most important way of showing love. Another gal I dated barely noticed or even cared that I bought her gifts. To her, buying things for the person you are dating isn't special enough because anyone can buy anything for anyone else, but spending quality time with your partner is far more meaningful.

I'm sure that you can come up with a few examples in your own romantic encounters where you tried everything in your power to show your partner that you love him or her and that you are genuinely interested in making the relationship stronger, but they just didn't get it. Many of us immediately start to think that our partner doesn't care about us as much or that we aren't good enough for them, but that is not true. In situations like these where your efforts seem like they get you nowhere, sit down with your partner and be open enough to ask about their history in love and family to find out what you can do to make them feel appreciated.

For years, I would jump from girlfriend to girlfriend trying to show my new girl that I appreciate her in the way that my old girlfriend wanted me to and it got me nowhere. This happens to most of us. If your loving efforts aren't appreciated you're probably trying to show your love in the way that your last partner would have appreciated and that is perfectly okay. That means that you are willing to change, learn and grow. You just have to learn how to tailor your growth in the direction that will be the most useful to you as well as your partner. Remember that loving another person is work but when you work, it works.

You and your partner have a great relationship with one another's family, you spend every single evening with each other and your schedules don't just include each other… you are an integral part of each other's schedule. Neither of you makes plans unless you consult with your significant other because neither of you wants to make the other feel left out. This is getting serious. It's been serious for quite some time now, but it is finally clear to both of you that after months and months to years of being together you both know that you are finally ready to take your relationship to the next level. It's time to take your relationship to the ultimate level.

Tonight, you two are out for a delicious dinner, attending a championship professional sporting event, or at a family gathering. Your partner gets the attention of every person in the room and a string quartet begins to play. Your partner tells everyone the story of how you two met back in the park, at the bar, in the library or reaching for the last cucumber in the grocery store and you get flustered. He or she gazes deeply into your eyes and says, "I just want to ask you here and now in front of everyone. Will you make me the happiest person alive and be with me for the rest of our lives?" The question has been popped. What happens now?

8
Dedication

Sooooo… your partner just popped the big question.
You two are about to spend the rest of your lives together.
Happily ever after has arrived and no fairy tale could
possibly capture the joy you feel at this very moment.
Your journey together will have some bumps along the way
and not every day is going to be a walk in the park, but you
can make it because you two love one another and are fully
dedicated to make this work. Sounds magical, doesn't it?
Well, if you are the majority of readers then I probably lost
you at this point.

Even if your love story has been written all the way up to
this point, at some time or another all of our love stories
have ended here. Suck your teeth, roll your eyes and sigh
away because I understand. Even if you are the small
percentage of readers that does believe forever is possible,
I'm sure that you know a great deal of people that don't
believe in this part of the love story. Love has changed.

This day and age, it's really hard to find someone that
meets your standards, shares your political views, has

ambition, wants what you want out of life and wants to
share that life with someone else. It's almost like the love
that our grandmother and grandfather's generation shared
doesn't exist anymore. Right? WRONG! That's not the
case at all and it's this way of thinking that makes
successful relationships difficult to find. We have become
so cynical that we do not view history with a rational mind.
In this chapter we are going to discuss the history of love
and marriage in a way that, hopefully, will change a mind or
two and help the world believe in love again!

The biggest myth that plagues romance today is the idea
that "these new generations" don't want to put forth the
effort for long lasting relationships and marriages. I
understand the concept because many of us have seen first
hand the power of a long lasting love in grandma and
grandpa's marriage, but there are far more factors at play
than we realize.

Firstly, I want to talk about the institution of marriage
itself. Ancient human societies needed a safe place for our
species to flourish. They needed a system of rules to
govern the ownership of property, protect the purity of
bloodlines and rear offspring. The institution of marriage
satisfied all of these requirements. In European societies,
the notion of romance as a reason for marriage did not
appear until medieval times.

In 866, Pope Nicholas I made a statement about unions,
"If the consent be lacking in a marriage, all other
celebrations, even should the union be consummated, are

rendered void," and that idea stands today. He spoke into existence the concept of 'I do', which is derived from the idea that both parties should be fully consenting to the marriage. To this day, although the majority of our modern society marries for genuine romantic interest, they also enter into marriage with its social and financial benefits in mind. Combining incomes, companionship, safety and security are a few of many reasons why people get married. If this is the case then the only difference between being eternal partners and being married should be the change in status from being single to married. With this in mind, I want to throw out the legally binding aspect of being married and instead focus on the relationship between eternally involved partners.

I believe that a woman must become a wife and a man must become a husband long before they decide to get married. Successfully married couples will all attest to the fact that one must be honest, understanding, patient, giving, and grateful for a marriage to last. Someone that doesn't have these virtues will not suddenly learn them simply because he or she decided to jump the broom. These traits are learned far before the wedding. It is critical to value these virtues because of how difficult it is to adjust to being with someone else forever.

Let's face it; for the majority of our adult lives we live with the freedom of making decisions, making purchases and meeting people without having to consider anyone else's opinion. When you declare that you are going to join into someone else's life, you are thrust into a brand new lifestyle where your choices and behavior directly affect your significant other. Although long-lasting love is a beautiful thing it is still a major adjustment in the beginning years and it requires both of you to be in sync with what you need from one another. Every day is a new opportunity to discover new aspects of your partner and also define familiar aspects of yourself. What makes you laugh? Does anything easily frustrate you? How do you receive criticism? Which parts of the day are you the most efficient? When do you like to take time to yourself? The list of questions is endless, so we need a way to make the process of figuring out these answers a little easier. We already have a way and it resides within the most basic aspect of our humanity… our system of values.

We forget very often that every man and woman was once an infant; a blank canvas onto which the world will paint an image of itself. Whether that painted image of the world is good or bad is based on what we experience but as infants our perceptions are purely based on instinct. When a baby is stimulated, that baby will respond accordingly and they only have two responses: pleasure or pain. If a baby gets tickled, feels hunger, hears a loud noise or sees a clown that baby is going to either accept or reject the stimulus.

As we grow and develop throughout life, we experience stimuli that we either accept or reject. The way that these stimuli are presented to us determines how our value system will be established. It is pretty confusing, but I am going to give an example so that it will all make sense.

One of my core values is the virtue of honesty. My mother raised me by teaching me about the world in all of its glory along with all of its horror so that I would fully understand what type of society I was living in. As a result of my mother being so honest with me, I have a deeply rooted appreciation for all those that show me the same level of uninhibited honesty. I do not tolerate dishonesty because essentially, someone that is willing to withhold the truth from me is telling me that they do not respect one of my core values. The presentation of this stimulus is painful to my developed instincts and I will always reject it.

You must first know what you value so that you can figure out what exactly you will and will not tolerate in a relationship. Once you figure that out, you need to share it with your partner so that boundaries can be established and ultimately, there will be no confusion about what is okay and what is not okay in the relationship. See **Exercise 7** in the appendix to try to evaluate your own value system.

Long-term relationships that are built on a foundation of understanding are much more likely to sustain the tests that will come over the course of your time together. We spend years operating by ourselves and even when we are in a dedicated relationship it is still difficult to transform our natural actions in order to make another person, a newcomer, more comfortable. All arguments stem from one partner violating a value of the other.

An argument about money isn't just about the rent/mortgage being late or a problem with excessive spending. The argument comes from a violation of one partner's value of safety and security. The partner that values safety and security has likely experienced stimuli that were caused by the understanding of or familiarity with living in a lower socioeconomic class. He or she will always defend the idea of a financially stable and secure lifestyle because even though a $200 pair of shoes may seem like nothing to his or her partner, that excessive or impulse purchasing behavior may eventually jeopardize the values of safety and security.

If we take the time to develop an understanding of our partner's values as well as those of our own early on, we can then make much better decisions about our thoughts, intentions and actions. Ultimately, the goal is to understand yourself as deeply as possible because only then can you become a considerate enough companion to sustain a relationship that lasts forever.

We find ourselves at yet another junction point in our story. Months have gone by. Years have gone by. You have successfully combined your schedules to the point where your eating and sleeping patterns match up perfectly. At this point, you live together and maybe you share a mutual love for a smaller life form that depends on the two of you for love and sustenance. Your wolf pack has grown by one and nothing can get in the way of that, but for some reason you two are arguing constantly and things have felt a bit shaky as of late. It's almost as if you two intentionally find things to fight about and they seem to happen over and over again. Your friends tell you that they are signs you need to jump ship, but you have no desire to leave. Before you make any rash decisions about leaving the person that you wanted to spend the rest of your life with a few months ago, you need to ask yourself… what are you afraid of?

Phase 3

Fear

9

Miscommunication

Before I start this chapter I would like to say that this last section of *My Sleeveless Heart* is the section that most of you will identify with the most. Even though we have all felt that yearning attraction from the first section and the burning sensation of love from the second section, we have all ended a relationship at one time or another. We remember the pain in our romantic lives much more easily than we remember the joy because we are conditioned to be critical of the negative aspects of life to avoid them in the future. I have a newsflash for you everyone. The more you think about the painful times, the more energy you put into your pain and that is going to continue to manifest itself in your life.

What I need from you is to think outside yourself from this point on. Don't think about the rest of this book as though I'm describing how our previous relationships ended. Think about it as me exploring how to make our next relationships better. Hopefully, in this way we can all go out into the world with optimism and hope so that the amazing person you strive to be every day will be recognized by all of the other people doing the exact same thing. Enjoy!

You can feel the connection between you and your love slowly slipping through your fingers. Neither of you know what is happening or why it started, but the elephant in the room is painfully obvious. Your relationship is on the rocks. What do you do now? It's very difficult when it comes to this point. You want to fight for your love but you don't want to fight with your love. Nobody wants to constantly argue about trivial matters but they seem to keep coming up. Leaving the toilet seat up, snoring too loudly, putting the toilet paper roll upside down, squeezing the toothpaste from the middle, dropping clothes and shoes all over the house, smacking food while chewing, eating with an open mouth, taking too long to get ready, neglecting to check on the baby, making large purchases without consulting one another, talking while a favorite show is on, liking provocative pictures on Instagram, lazing around all day without trying to find a job…

Have I struck a nerve here with anyone? These are only a fraction of the ridiculously long list of stupid things that we fight with each other about in our relationships. Even major arguments about things like infidelity, addiction or family drama can be lessened or completely eliminated with a mutual respect for proper communication.

Communication is key in life in general. In order to survive you have to be able to communicate with the world around you. The same goes for surviving in a relationship. Just like the world, though, relationship communication has several different languages and you must be fluent in the communicative language that your partner speaks. An English speaking person in a small town in Eastern Germany where many people do not speak in English would have a more difficult experience than someone that speaks in German.

A person that does not know how his or her partner receives information will have just as much trouble. In the arguments listed above, one partner is trying to communicate with the other to get a particular task done but there always seems to be a language barrier. Arguments are started out of the frustration from not being able to communicate effectively and I have some thoughts on why this happens.

If I wanted to order a cheeseburger at a fast food restaurant, I would say, "I would like to order a cheeseburger," plain and simple with no ifs, ands or buts about it. I know exactly what I want and I ask for it but in order to guarantee that the order is prepared correctly and the employee feels appreciated, I have to ask for it a certain way. The same thing applies to a request in a relationship and I feel as though our requests go unheeded because we sometimes don't directly request what we want. I think it's because we just don't want to sound rude and make the other person feel inferior, but we all do something that I call *inquisitive direction* when we want our partner to do something. We ask a question and imply that we want an action performed. Here's an example from my own experience so it's easier to understand:

Her: "Are those your dishes in the sink?"
Me: "Yeah, I just had some spaghetti."
Her: "Shouldn't you wash them before we go to bed?"
Me: "Meh, I'm kinda tired, I'll do it in the morning. Besides, they could use a good soak."
Her: "Wouldn't it be easier to just do it now?"

See what I mean? She is telling me to get up and do the dishes without actually saying it. We ALL do this in our own way and the question usually makes it sound like it's not the asker's idea. She made it as though she was asking me if I thought it would be a good idea to wash the dishes tonight. If I wash the dishes, she won't feel as though she's nagging me to do it because at that moment, she transferred the idea to make it sound like it was mine. The problem is that in scenarios like this, the dishes won't get done because she hasn't requested that they be washed. She will then harbor resentment because I've made her feel that I don't value her desire and in time, she is going to explode on me about it because I've been disrespecting her opinion for a long time without even knowing it.

Think about every time someone has lost it on you about something small. Did they make it sound like you've been doing that small thing for a long time? Can you remember them directly asking you to stop doing it? Probably not. Now, think about every time you've lost it on somebody for them doing something small that irritated you. Had they been doing that something small for a long time? Did you directly ask them to stop doing it? Probably not. If you did sit him or her down and directly ask for what you wanted and didn't get it, then you were/are dating a jerk and you needed/need that relationship to end. Ask for what you want and you can discuss it as a couple in a partnership. No one is going to read your mind; so be understanding, patient and honest. If your partner is the same you will come to a mutual conclusion. Many readers may be wondering how to ask in order to get results. Let's talk about it.

It's going to take some serious reforming of us as people to be comfortable with being transparent to our partners. We are all so focused on how difficult it can be to truly be you with someone else that we walk around with emotional walls to protect our feelings. The problem with emotional walls is that no one can get in and you can't get out. Breaking down these walls comes from proper communication and making sure that your partner knows as much about you as possible.

When it comes to making requests for action like we discussed above, we need to apply the same openness to both partners involved. Let's use my dishwashing story as an example. My girlfriend in this scenario prefers that the kitchen, living room and bedroom be totally clean before going to bed. I agree that it definitely feels better when everything is clean when you wake up. However, the real reason why she was always so adamant about it is that while she was growing up she would get into serious trouble with her mother if everything wasn't spotless in the morning.

That upbringing caused her to develop a need to have everything clean in order to satisfy that part of her mother in her subconscious so that she won't get into "trouble". Anxiety was implanted in her psyche and made her unable to sleep before everything was clean because of years of fearing her mother's next morning consequences. Like I said earlier in the book, we spend years behaving our own way before we try to mix lives with someone else. In my case, our lifestyles clashed and that caused a conflict between us. The first step to fixing it is to have open and honest talks often.

We are continuously evolving people and your partner needs to know who you are at all times. Sit down every so often and talk about what you've been feeling. Check in with your partner to see how they received the love you'd shown them throughout that month or to explain why you haven't shown them any love at all. Once you have established an open channel of proper communication, the next step is to share with your partner as much information about what makes you unhappy.

We can get so focused on making sure our partners know how to make us happy that we don't make sure they know how not to piss us off. Once they know what bothers you, you need to come to an agreement about how to avoid situations where your irritations could potentially arise. Now that you've been armed with the truth, let's get back to the dishes. With this new method of openness, let's erase the conversation she and I had earlier and try it the open way:

Her: "Are those your dishes in the sink?"
Me: "Yeah, I just had some spaghetti."
Her: "We agreed that we would have the kitchen clean before we go to bed."
Me: "Meh, I'm kinda tired, I'll do it in the morning. Besides, they could use a good soak."
Her: "We agreed that we would have the kitchen clean before we go to bed."

PERIOD! Even if I came back with that foolishness about the dishes needing to soak, it still wouldn't change the fact that we agreed on the kitchen being clean before going to sleep. In the new scenario she reminds me that it was a choice that we made as a couple to make sure that her preference to have the kitchen clean is fulfilled. This response is only effective if you have the honesty talk and if the word choice "we agreed" is very specific. More often than not, when an agreement is reached, the sentence starts off with either, "I thought I said," or, "didn't you say."

Humans are very particular when it comes to giving and receiving criticism for doing something wrong. In life, it seems that we want all the credit when things go right and none of the blame when things go wrong. In both cases, especially when it comes to an issue like this one, we have to ignore credit and blame and focus on responsibility. You as a couple are responsible for the decisions that you make together, so instead of taking the credit by starting with, "I thought I said…" or passing the blame by starting with, "didn't you say…" share the responsibility by starting with, "we agreed that…"

Let's go back to the beginning of these ridiculous arguments and assume that you didn't have an open and honest channel of communication (because most of us don't). Let's assume that you go back and forth with one another about what your partner has done wrong and how much they have upset you in recent times. Let's just say that you feel neglected, disrespected or flat out lied to. Well folks, at the root of all those feelings, the underlying reason that you are arguing is the fact that one or both of you does not fully appreciate what you have.

10

Unappreciation

You're at each other's throats for reasons neither of you can remember days later. The spark in your relationship only seems to ignite when you have angry make up sex after one of you apologizes for being a jerk and yet, that's still not enough. Your anger festers inside you throughout the day and when you see one another, the silence is deafening. What is going on here? Why are you fighting so much? It can't really about the socks that got left in the middle of the living room floor or the random late night phone call from the ex can it? Absolutely not.

Not one of the problems that you're experiencing in your relationship is as simple as the thing you're fighting about. There's a difference between a problem and an issue and we need to learn how to get to the root of the issue. I have some thoughts about how these issues develop over time and what we can do to stop them in their tracks before they create problems.

For someone that loves cars or jewelry, it would be pretty easy to appreciate a Lykan Hypersport or an

Audemars Piguet Royal Oak. Knowing their beauty and value creates a feeling of excitement, desire and attachment when either of these enthusiasts comes across an item of such grandeur. Let's say these lovers of cars and jewelry finally get to own that car or that watch. Over time, their appreciation is going to decrease because once our enthusiasts owned the items, the allure and desire to possess the items disappear.

The car lover will get comfortable enough to eat in the car, drive a little more recklessly and wash it less frequently. The watch lover will get comfortable enough to forget to put the watch back in the watch valet, check the time on his or her cell phone and set the watch with the dial facing down. Every person does this to personal inanimate objects like watches, cars, clothes, etc., but we also have to realize that we have a habit of doing it to the *object* of our affection; our romantic interest.

The thrill of the chase and the beginning phases of getting to know each other seem to be the most fun times because everything is new. Our appreciation for him or her is still very high. Feeling unappreciated can actually be rooted in our partners neglecting to show the same type of interest and pay us the same amount of attention they did when the relationship started.

Human beings are social creatures and we all require attention to be socially functional. Within a relationship, we expect the undivided attention of our significant other. That is the only evidence we have to prove affection and exclusivity. When we get to a point in our relationships where we are arguing constantly about even the smallest things, I believe that it stems from the fear of losing the connection because there isn't enough attention being received. Your car isn't going to feel unappreciated if you don't wash it for two weeks, but your significant other will certainly write a "Wash Me" message in their dirt if they feel neglected. That message is usually expressed through confrontation and conflict because it is hard to figure out how to get someone you love to pay attention to you. This frustration is what causes problems. Interestingly enough, we have a defense mechanism to alleviate that frustration and make ourselves feel like our partner is paying attention to us. It's a type of attention that many of us require in order to feel secure. Obedience.

In every relationship, you establish rules and behaviors by discussing them with your significant other but there are also rules that are not discussed and yet still expected. The dominant personality is usually the one that writes these unwritten rules by forcing their expectations onto their partner in a theory that I call the "Soil and Seed" theory. In the "Soil and Seed" theory, one partner is the soil, the other partner is the seed, water is the strength of the relationship, sunlight is reality, weather is emotional state and the flower is the success of the relationship.

A seed is small and powerful with the potential to change into something spectacular but they are easily moved and must be placed in the proper conditions in order to grow.

The seed in the relationship is the partner that is more dominating and in their need to be comfortable in order to flourish, they become susceptible to agitation and aggression. This person demands specificity or else they will feel as though their needs are not respected and they will feel easily misunderstood and unappreciated.

Soil is grounded and easily malleable but soil must create the appropriate conditions necessary for growth. The soil in the relationship does whatever is necessary to avoid conflict, yields to the needs of their partner and is willing to make large personality and behavioral changes in order to make the relationship work. This person is usually the quieter and more supportive partner, but over time they allow themselves to get used and begin to feel unappreciated and devalued because of how much they've changed themselves to satisfy their seed.

The water serves as the strength of the relationship because both partners need time to affirm that they are involved in something that will grow into something better. The weather conditions serve as the emotional state of both parties involved in the relationship including the baggage that we all carry from our previous relationships. Sunlight serves as reality in the fact that we are programmed to believe in love the way we see it in movies which means that love in the real world will not be clouded (pun intended) by false ideas and scenarios.

When you put a seed in soil, add water and sunlight with the right weather conditions, a flower will grow but it will have difficulty blooming if either of these elements doesn't do its job. A flaw in personality, emotional state or perception of reality is the root (pun intended) of one or both partners feeling unappreciated, which stems (pun intended) from attention deficiency.

Any one of the components in the growth of our love flower can be counterproductive to its growth if it doesn't function the way it should. Unrealistic expectations and impatience can block the sunlight that shines truth into the relationship. The water that feeds belief in the longevity of the relationship can be too much (which will make your love feel clingy and forced) or too little (which can make you skeptical of your love's authenticity). The weather that brings changing emotional states and previous emotional baggage can require an unexpected emergency action plan that may have never been discussed or rehearsed. Sunlight, weather and water conditions aside, the seed and the soil have the hardest job in making the love flower bloom because their relationship must be an equal give and take. Therefore, when either the seed or the soil expects to receive more than they are willing to give, the flower will not grow properly.

If you are more of a seed type then you are very likely giving, outgoing and you really do not like when you don't get things your way. You tend to put the needs of others before your own and it gives you a sense of control to know that others truly benefit from having you in their life. The seed expects more than they are willing to give by trying to get their soil to think and act the same way they do. This type of individual acts out in aggressive, nagging and nit picky ways in order to change an undesired behavior in their partner. When a seed reacts with a tantrum or outburst, they are actually using negative reinforcement techniques to put a subconscious block on that behavior or action in the mind of their soil.

For example, I am a soil type. I pretty much go with the flow and I can pretty easily adapt to the conditions around me in order to keep the peace. My seed loved me and I knew it. However, she was completely opposed to hearing about me having sex with another woman in a story. I believe now that since she had been cheated on so many times before me, even the thought of me having sex with someone else brought up feelings of insecurity and jealousy. We would get into a huge fight about who the girl is, where she is now, how long it's been since I'd spoken to her, etc. Even though I didn't understand why it was such a problem, the negative reinforcement technique caused me to withhold any stories, ideas or conversations about other women even if they were just friends or coworkers. Even pleasant conversations with strangers that I would have normally wanted to share with her I kept to myself because I didn't want her to think that I was being unfaithful.

At the same time, she loved how comfortable she felt being able to talk to me about her past sexual escapades or funny stories about men flirting with her on the street. It didn't bother me at first, but over time I started to get irritated and uneasy when she talked about other men. I wasn't jealous, I was more upset that she had the audacity to expect something that she never gave.

No matter what the condition of the soil, the seed type tries to dig its roots in to anchor itself. The biggest issue for the seed type is that they have a tendency to try and force everyone around them to see the world through their eyes without giving the time to listen and understand the worldview of other people. Seeds believe that the potential they bring gives them power over the relationship and allows them freedom to receive more than they give but seeds must realize that they must be adaptive and understanding in order for the relationship flower to grow harmoniously and without unbalanced force and control.

If you are more of a soil type then you are likely a good listener, very supportive and easily adapt to the moods of the people around you. You tend to be someone that gives of yourself without expecting any acknowledgement even though you sometimes secretly yearn for that validation. The soil doubts and often suppresses their opinions and beliefs in order to conform to the desires of their seed. This type of individual is susceptible to changing personality traits about themselves so often that eventually they will be in a position where they don't know who they are anymore.

In this way, a soil type will at some point become barren and unable to sustain healthy growth because of his or her past encounters. If water is the strength of the relationship over time, then a partner being too clingy and needy will flood the soil because you are trying to force the flower to grow before it's ready to. The next seed that tries to plant itself will be viewed extra critically if it tries to sow its roots too strong or too fast. If fire is a traumatizing life event, then a partner that does not emotionally understand the soil type can scorch the earth. The next seed that tries to plant itself will not have an emotionally available place to grow. If salt is a violation of the relationship's rules such as: infidelity, domestic violence or insensitivity, then a partner that commits such an offense will purposefully change the composition of the ground. The next seed that tries to plant itself will be trying to grow in a poisoned ground that is unable to nurture new life.

The biggest issue with the soil type is that they have a habit of holding grudges and find it difficult to truly forgive the transgressions of their past. Soil types need to learn to view each new seed as an individual that has nothing to do with what happened with the previous seeds. Every seed is different which means that each one that tries to plant itself needs to be treated with respect because the possibilities of what will grow out of nurturing soil are endless. Soil types have to figure out how to stand up for what they believe and not be such people pleasers. When you sacrifice who you are to satisfy someone else, you are endangering your self worth and will ultimately be overrun by your partner because they know you will do anything they ask you to do.

In your relationships, are you the seed or are you the soil? Growth happens through conflict but even in conflict we can still learn how to become a better person in the relationship. When we are in an equal partnership, it's much easier to be happy. If you give as much as you expect to receive, then that balance will bring your relationship harmony. The main thing that needs to be given brings us back to the topic of this chapter. Attention. PAY ATTENTION! Think about it, if you pay as much attention to your partner as you expect them to pay attention to you, then you will be fully aware of what your partner wants, needs and expects. With that awareness, you will get along much better and it will be very much appreciated.

Sadly, that is much easier said than done and in all of our lives, we have been in situations where things don't get any better. That feeling of being unappreciated does not go away and neither of you seems to want to take the first step in order to remedy the problem. Maybe you just aren't right for each other or you truly were not ready for this relationship to last forever. Either way, you know that the next step is to get away from this person before you do or say something you'll regret. You've had this conversation with yourself long enough and it's about time to sever this tie and set your partner free.

11

Severance

Maybe you take your lover to a public place so that you feel safe. Maybe you sit them down at home so that you don't have strangers in your business. Maybe you're not that brave and you send a text message or an email. However you decide to handle your business, you know that today is the day that you are going to end this relationship. Whatever your reason, you have been thinking about this for quite some time now. The nervous feeling in the pit of your stomach feels strangely similar to the feeling you remember from when they first walked up to you. Now, that feeling is not from the thrill of connection but the fear of separation.

Nobody wants to break up but sometimes we have to. In every relationship that ends, there is a breaker and a broken. I don't believe in the idea of a breakup being "mutual". Even though they may both agree to the circumstances one of them has to have initiated the conversation. Most breakups are not mutual though, so how do we try to understand why couples split up? All of us have rooted for at least one couple that looks so great together it's hard to imagine them ever breaking up so why did they? How could she have been so violent toward him? He loved her. How could he have cheated on her? She loved him. Why were they so worried about money? They had more than enough. I don't have all the answers, but I want to talk about some of the most common reasons why couples split up. Hopefully we can discuss the underlying issues that made these people give up on something that was once so beautiful.

Chris Rock said it best, "Think about the amount of time you've been together. Now cut that in half. That's how long you've been breaking up." In the beginning of this book and the start of this romantic encounter everything was fun and laughs, but at some point something changed. Was it you? Was it them? The short answer is neither. Both of you are the same person you were when this whole thing started. Now that time has gone by you are seeing your partner for the person they are instead of the person they wanted you to see and the person you thought they were.

Your personality conflicts hadn't been a problem until you truly began to see and show your personalities to each other. With this I mind, I want to talk about a few of the major reasons why couples break up. I want to make very clear that people are way too sensitive in an impractical and self-centered way when it comes to relationship-ending conflicts. Let's say that a girlfriend cheats. She didn't have sex with someone else just to hurt her partner's feelings.

She wanted to have sex with someone else and in turn, she hurt her partner. Let's say that a boyfriend lies. He didn't lie just to hurt his partner's feelings. He wanted to experience the thing he lied about while still keeping his partner's love and adoration.

Very few people that have been hurt by their partner have been the focus of the action that hurt them. With this in mind, we need to think more about the mentality of the person that commits these violations of the relationship's rules and why they were unable to control their urges and personality flaws in a hurtful manner. In doing so, we are going to discuss physical and mental abuse, infidelity, lying and love for money over love for the partner.

Within abusive relationships, believe it or not, abusers and their abused are both victims, but at different times. The abused are the current victims, but the abusers were victims long before the relationship started. The women and men that hurt their partners were all devastatingly hurt in their young lives and that's the only way they know how to function. They carry the weight of their childhood mistreatment and that powerlessness resurfaces in their romantic lives. It's about control.

As children, our perceptions of us and the world around us are very strongly based on how our parental figures treat us and what they teach us about ourselves; whether it's true or not. Some parental figures tell their children that they are worthless, pathetic, incompetent and weak. I fell madly in love with a woman that is the most beautiful, intelligent, funny, witty, giving and sexy woman I have ever met. However, for thirty years her mother woke her up every day yelling at her about how useless she is, how worthless she is, how much of a whore she is, etc. In turn, my genuine compliments fell on deaf ears because she was unable to believe that her qualities were even true. Come to find out, her mother had been mentally and physically abused in her childhood and the way she was talked to is how she talked to her child. As a child, no matter how much it hurts to receive such horrible treatment these abused children have to deal with it because they have no power. They still depend on their abusive parental figures for food, clothing and shelter.

When they become adults, I believe that the repeat of their vicious abusive cycle comes from the urge to make up for all the years of powerlessness. Think about it. If a child is raised poor and they win the lottery, they are going to buy everything they ever wanted because they couldn't before the money came. In this analogy, the money is emotional power. Someone that has never had any power in their life will grow up yearning for the chance to feel powerful and the only way they know how to feel more power over someone is the way their parental figure took power away from them; physical and mental abuse. If you find yourself with someone like this, you need to know that it is not anything against you or your value.

Your partner does not abuse you because you are invaluable. They treat you the way they do because they are trying to satisfy an emotional void within themselves. If you are not willing to tolerate such treatment, you need to escape that situation before things get dangerous. If you think that treatment is okay, then you need to look back at your childhood and realize you are falling back into a familiar pattern that you should be trying to get away from. No person should ever be made to feel lower than his or her partner. Power over the emotional state of a relationship should never rest in one person's words or hands so you must be willing to stand up for yourself in situations that your partner tries to make you feel inferior.

Infidelity. Jeez. How many of you have been waiting to get to this paragraph? Let me start by apologizing to every person out there that has ever been cheated on. You are right to feel the way you do because they did you wrong. You are more than enough. You are special. You are amazing. With that said, I want to continue by saying that they did not cheat on you the way you think. They had sex with someone else for themselves, not against you. No one cheats with the intention of hurting his or her partner. Their intrigue was just stronger than their loyalty. In a situation where someone becomes unfaithful it is because the cheater isn't ready for the type of relationship that is expected of him or her. Because of this fact, I want to talk specifically about why men cheat.

It has been my observation that women cheat because of emotional starvation, curiosity, the possibility of personal gain or any of a multitude of different reasons. A majority of men cheat because the thrill of sexually conquering multiple women is difficult to suppress in the mind of a man. Let me make something clear, I'm not saying that men are unable to keep it in their pants. I'm saying that we are not raised to think that our sexuality is something to treasure the way that women are.

Little girls are taught to keep their private parts to themselves. They are taught that boys only want one thing and so they have to guard their special areas from the sexual urges and advances of little boys. As teenagers, young women are taught that their virginity is sacred and should only be given to someone that deserves it. Men, on the other hand, are not taught to view our bodies with such purity.

Teenage boys and teenage girls have the same urges. Since the girls are taught to keep their sexual treasure guarded for the one person that's worth it, the boys grow up thinking that pursuit and conquest of said treasure is the key to manhood. Even listen to the language we use with virginity. When you refer to a woman having sex for the first time, the question is, "Who took your virginity?" implying that she gave it to someone who took it from her. It sounds controlled and beautiful. Ask a man and the question is, "Who did you lose your virginity to?" implying that his virginity was all over the place available for anyone to take. It sounds like we're helpless because psychologically, we are.

By the time we're men we have had such little practice with sexual self-control that even in a relationship, it's still difficult to deny another woman's advances. Every man has to find it in his own self-worth to be a faithful man. Not to his partner, but to himself. When a man finally understands that his sexuality is valuable and that sharing his body is special, his urge to sexually conquer every woman he sees will drastically decrease. Ultimately he will become the type of man that only wants to give himself to one person.

Lying is an interesting topic because as much as we shout to the hills how much we hate liars, every single day, every person on this planet tells at least one lie. We can call it a little white lie, stretching the truth, fibbing, beating around the bush, concealing the truth all we want to. We still lie. It only hurts when our partner lies to us in a way that conceals something they know we wouldn't appreciate. It especially hurts when our partner lies to us because it takes away our choice to either understand or be upset.

I lied to a girl I dated and I had to look inside myself when she called me out on it. I came over to her house after a work banquet where I was accompanied by an attractive female friend I'd slept with before. My friend called me while I was cuddling on the couch to make sure I made it safely and the call made my romantic interest curious. "Why didn't you take me tonight? Have you two had sex before? Why haven't I met her?" My friend was also my business function companion because I'd seen her behave in a social business setting, but the tone in my interest's voice was very unsettled.

I immediately blurted out, "No we've never had sex," knowing that it was a lie. I believed in my mind that she would not be happy knowing that my friend and I had a sexual history and I lied in order to tell her what I thought she wanted to hear. The problem with telling your partner what you think they want to hear opposed to telling them the truth is that you are taking away their choice to understand and be okay with the truth or to reject it and be upset at you. Telling the truth is doing your part. It's up to them to deal with it. In situations where you tell the truth and your partner still gives you grief, there is likely an underlying issue your partner has with you or with themselves and you need to open a channel of proper communication to discuss the issue.

Money can play a huge factor in ending a relationship if spending behaviors and responsibilities between partners are not balanced. Financial security is a very important part of our society and there are several ways to threaten your partner's comfort with your financial security as a couple. A partner that seldom offers to pay for outings and necessities can cause financial stress. Usually the partner that makes more money is expected to be the one to pay for dates in the beginning but as time goes forward that partner can feel as if their financial contribution is expected instead of appreciated.

Through it all we each experience situations that we are unable or unwilling to work through. When the time comes that a relationship needs to end you must remember that your strength and your pride is all you will have in the coming days, but you must also be willing to understand what really happened. You must be honest with yourself what your partner contributed to the break up and also what you contributed. In order to become a better person in your next relationship, you need to take all of the offenses and transgressions you both committed in the relationship and forgive your partner and yourself for them.

12

Forgiveness

You have been away from the love of your life for several days, months, maybe even years. Everything about life feels a little bit different since your relationship ended. Whether those differences are helpful or harmful, you know that things are different. A large chunk of your time that was previously spent with one person is now open for you to figure out on your own.

If they initiated the breakup and you didn't suspect the end of your relationship, you might have a lingering feeling of resentment. If they initiated the breakup and you could feel it coming, you might feel as though you were set free in order to develop more as a person without your ex hindering your personal growth. If you initiated the breakup because you needed space to understand some new attributes about yourself, you might have a sweeping pride in your bravery for choosing your own happiness over the happiness of someone else. If you initiated the breakup because you needed to get out of a potentially dangerous situation, there may be a lingering fear of retaliation but you should also feel a sense of empowerment and personal responsibility. If you initiated the breakup because you just wanted to be single again, you probably don't feel anything.

Whoever initiated the breakup and for whatever reason, you two are no longer together. That may be for now and it may be forever, but at this moment in the end of the book you are as single as you were in the beginning. This chapter about forgiveness is not necessarily about asking for forgiveness but about forgiving yourself and internally forgiving your ex. The goal is to allow you to heal from the offenses that were committed in your relationship so that you can have a better view on the way you experience love in your next relationship; even if it's back with your ex.

The first step is to be honest with yourself about what happened in the relationship that caused it to end. What did your ex do and what did you do? Yes, you had a contribution to the problems in the relationship even if you think you're innocent. A huge misconception in relationships is the idea that forgiveness is letting go of past transgressions.

Whenever there is an offense in the relationship, there is the offender and the offended. People have such a hard time forgetting about past negative experiences that it's safe to say the offended will never get over the offense. Whether the offense be infidelity, physical or mental abuse, disrespect, a bold faced lie, that event is never going to be forgotten no matter how much time has passed or how much the offender behaves. It's not necessarily because the offended thinks their offender will repeat the behavior. It's literally because the action or behavior committed by the offender will get stored in the memory of the offended.

The same thing goes for the first ice cream date, the first kiss or the first time making love. A critical offense is a major shift in the dynamic of the relationship and therefore cannot be forgotten. Therefore, the feelings felt by the offended will never be forgotten because those feelings were tied to the events and circumstances that led up to the offense. I want to give an example because it's pretty confusing.

I lied to my ex. I was out of town for work and I planned to meet up with a rather attractive female acquaintance without telling her. I called my ex at 10:30 with no answer and texted her goodnight at 11 with my phone on silent. I didn't answer my phone all night long. When she found out through social media that I hung out with my female friend and asked about it, with an accusatory tone, I panicked and lied saying that we saw each other at random. When my ex found out that hanging out with my friend was actually planned and I lied about it, we had a huge fallout but she forgave me. Or so I thought.

Later on in our relationship when I was away for work again, my phone legitimately died late at night and I had no access to a charger. The next time we spoke, she legitimately believed that I hid a sexual encounter with a different female acquaintance with no evidence or reason to believe the encounter happened other than suspicion. Even though time may have passed, my offense was not forgotten so we need to talk about how to work through those feelings.

The short answer is to stop telling yourself that you'll ever get over how you felt because you won't. When someone in a relationship gets hurt, that pain will eventually subside and eventually it can get suppressed, but I truly believe that it is impossible to completely let go of previous hurt. I don't think that the offended actually forgives. I think that the offender simply avoids the events and circumstances that lead up to the offense so that the feeling does not resurface.

Let's say that I was having an extramarital affair, but I used the excuse "I was working late" to commit my infidelities. If I got caught, I was truly sorry for a stupid mistake and my spouse forgave me, that would be a miracle. If I ever tried to tell her that I was working late again she would expect that I take every measure possible to prove that I was doing what I said. Working.

Overcoming an obstacle as a couple is possible, but the thought that the problems it created will ever go away is a myth. If the offender is truly apologetic, then they fully understand the grief and pain they put their partner through. Therefore, the offender is going to do everything they can to behave in a way that does not remind the offended partner of the betrayal and hurt they experienced when the offense was initially committed. If you have been wronged in your relationship, you must understand that your partner did not do what they did to hurt you intentionally.

Every choice that we make in life is to make ourselves happy and we do the best we can to make the people we love happy in the process, but sometimes we fall short. The hurtful part about relationships is that there are just some things that our partners still do for themselves even though they know it will hurt us if we ever found out. That's just the nature of long-term relationships. We need to learn how to turn the focus away from ourselves when we feel hurt and try thinking about why our offending partner felt compelled to do what they did to hurt us. There is an underlying reason to everything we do as humans, especially in relationships, and for a long-term relationship to succeed or for a single person to find closure there must be that understanding. A big step in that process is being able to forgive your partner, your exes and yourself.

There is a big difference between an apology and remorse. An apology is when you say that you have remorse for something you said or did. Remorse is when you are truly sorry for something you've said or done. Our society leads us to believe that someone is remorseful when they give an apology. An apology is treated like the most difficult thing to do. "The hardest thing to do in a relationship is to say you're sorry." NO!!! The hardest thing to do in a relationship is to actually BE sorry and put forth the energy and effort to fix it. To say you're sorry and not mean it is an insult to the intelligence of your partner and we are going to talk about why.

First of all, the only true apology is remedy. If I'm truly sorry for doing something I shouldn't have, I'll take it upon myself not to do it again. Many people apologize simply to make themselves feel better that they offered an apology. Let's say I am about to tell my girlfriend a story that I've told a hundred times. Before I tell the story I start with, "I'm sorry if you've already heard this but I have to tell it again," and I continue to tell the same story. Am I really sorry? Hell no I'm not sorry. If I was sorry, then I would have the self control and restraint to not tell the story. The same goes for the people that curse inappropriately, abuse their spouses, overstay their welcome, take more than they're offered or anyone else that apologizes for doing something they continue to do.

An apology is supposed to be used for situations where an offense is committed and it is an accident that the offended party could not stop from happening. I'm going to use backing into a car and stepping on someone's toe as examples. If I step on your toe, I'm going to apologize because I know that you wouldn't have been able to stop your toe from getting stepped on. If I back into your car with my car, I'm going to apologize because I know that you wouldn't have been able to avoid your car from getting hit. This must mean that when I say "I'm sorry" I'm telling the person I offended that they were unable to control the situation. I am sorry for putting them in an uncomfortable situation and my apology says that they are powerless to stop the offense from happening like getting their toe stepped on or getting their car backed into. Right? Now let's take this information back to telling my girlfriend the same story a thousand times.

When I apologize to her for telling the same story and I still tell it, what I'm really saying is that I'm sorry she doesn't have the will power or control to stop me from telling the story. I know that she has ALLOWED me to tell the same story over and over again and I can tell that she doesn't want to hear it but I know that she won't stop me. That apology is empty because I'm not sorry for telling the story but for her being unable to stop me from telling it.

Bringing this back to more serious issues within relationships, a wife that beats her husband (yes it happens, way more than you think) and always says she's sorry for it isn't apologizing for beating her husband. If she was sorry, she'd stop. She's apologizing FOR her husband that he doesn't have the strength or control of the situation to stop her from putting her hands on him. Looking back on your relationships think about all the times that someone offended you in some way on a regular basis but they always apologized for it. If the behavior didn't change then they were not truly sorry.

As time goes on and the offense continues to happen, the apology becomes less valuable until eventually you don't believe it anymore. That's because it didn't hold any merit in the first place. You need to examine what about your partner and your relationship gave them the idea that they could continue to commit the offense they kept apologizing for. Anyone I know that has ever put their foot down and said enough is enough never had to deal with that offensive behavior again.

If you continuously apologize in your relationship, and even in life, you need to examine what you are apologizing for. Most of the time when someone habitually apologizes it's because they experienced a relationship that they were made to feel incapable, inferior and belittled. If you are truly sorry for something then you shouldn't have to say it out loud every time it happens. You need to seriously look inside yourself and figure out whether you need to change something, fix something or simply leave the person/situation you are apologizing for.

Remember, if an apology is given because the offended can't do anything about it then you need to know for certain that you want to stop doing the thing that they can't change. Stand up for what you believe in. Stand up for what you want to do. Stand up for who you want to be in life. Be yourself without apologizing because then you're assuming the people around you don't want you to be yourself but are too powerless to stand up for themselves.

Whether you are bitterly single or happily married, your

romantic destiny is completely based on your ability to forgive; forgiving those who have wronged you and forgiving yourself for those you have wronged. Although there may be similarities among the people you've dated each individual is different when it comes to your love life. If you treat your next the way you treated your ex you are asking for confusion and chaos because the only way to make a relationship work is to have an open mind and an open heart.

We must teach ourselves how to love unconditionally. Every day I see posts on social media from those crying out for love with no knowledge of how to find it for themselves. The first step is to love you more than anyone else. The most unconditional love that any of us should have is the love for our own self with all of our quirks, perks, flaws, triumphs and fears. Self love will make you complete and only complete people make truly happy and successful couples.

Sure you want to find someone that compliments you. Look for someone that will encourage you to work harder, not do your work for you. Seek someone that will make you smile, not serve as the only source of your happiness. Sometimes we all need someone to be there to serve as an emotional crutch when times get tough and I get that, but when they become your wheelchair you both lose.

If I can give one piece of advice I will say that I want you to learn how to just be. You have evolved into the wonderful person that you are because of ALL the events and experiences of your past. You are going to continue to evolve into an even more wonderful person because of ALL the experiences you are going to have. Knowing this, you must realize that everything about you is purposed and perfect, so just *be* yourself. We are all called human *be*ings for a reason. We are not human actings, waitings, wishings, wantings, playings, cryings, we are human *be*ings. Who you are is exactly who you are supposed to *be*. If you can accept and appreciate today for all of its glory and tragedy, you will *be*come a better person *be*cause you are simply *be*ing yourself. We all have a say so in how our love lives will turn out and it's impossible to know how someone else will play a part in it, but if you take anything away from this book remember this… love is work, but it works.

Exercise

Appendix

Exercise 1
What is Your Type?

Write out the names of three to five people that you were romantically involved with.

_____ _____ _____ _____ _____

Underneath each name, write out up to 10 physical features, things they describe themselves as, things that stood out to you or things you feel had a significant impact on their personality.

_____ _____ _____ _____ _____

_____ _____ _____ _____ _____

_____ _____ _____ _____ _____

_____ _____ _____ _____ _____

_____ _____ _____ _____ _____

_____ _____ _____ _____ _____

_____ _____ _____ _____ _____

_____ _____ _____ _____ _____

_____ _____ _____ _____ _____

_____ _____ _____ _____ _____

If more than half of these characteristics match, then this likely means one of two things. This personality profile is either your type or simply the type of person that you attract.

Thinking Points
-Is this your preferred type?
-Are you currently with someone that matched this type?
-Are you happy with you relationship status?
-What changed in your life throughout the time that these relationships happened?
-What characteristics about yourself seek or attract this type?

If less than half to none of these characteristics match among your names then you likely don't have a type or you are still figuring out what you want for your life.

Thinking Points
-Why did you get involved with each of these people?
-What changed in your life between involving yourself with each of the names listed?
-Which name/type did you enjoy the most?
-Did you ever have something to prove to yourself or someone else? If so, why?
-Are you currently involved with anyone similar to either of your listed names?
-Are you happy with your relationship status?

Exercise 2
State your Intentions

Choose your most successful or enjoyable relationship.
Use the memories of this relationship to fill in the
following phrases:

While I was with _____ my primary
focus in life was _____. I did my
best to contribute _____ to the
relationship and in return I most often received
_____. In the beginning the thing
we did together the most was
_____. I changed
_____ about myself and felt the
need to sacrifice _____ to keep the
relationship healthy. I was _____
encouraged to _____ for myself and
I succeeded at _____ while I was
with _____.

Thinking Points

-How many times has someone outright told you what he or she wanted and it turned you off?

-What do you want out of a relationship with someone?

-How many times have you expressed your intentions openly and it was well received?

-What have you done in the past to get what you want out of a relationship?

-If you got exactly what you wanted from the beginning, would your intentions evolve, would you become bored from conquest or would you exit altogether since there is nothing else that can be gained?

-How many times have you gotten exactly what you originally wanted from a relationship?

Exercise 3
How Embarrassing

Think about five different events in your life that were absolutely humiliating and were not funny when they happened but you can laugh at them now. Give each story a creative and hilarious title if you haven't already.

_____ _____ _____ _____ _____

Think of people you've dated or potentially wanted to date and put their name to one or more of the stories you didn't tell them, but you believe they would think it's funny the way you do. Use the sentence provided with the name in the first blank and the story name in the second blank.

_____ would think _____ was funny
_____ would think _____ was funny
_____ would think _____ was funny
_____ would think _____ was funny
_____ would think _____ was funny
_____ would think _____ was funny
_____ would think _____ was funny
_____ would think _____ was funny
_____ would think _____ was funny
_____ would think _____ was funny
_____ would think _____ was funny

<u>Thinking Points</u>

-How did you get over the embarrassment of each of these events?

-Who have you told these stories to?

-Why haven't you told these stories to the people you wrote down?

-Will you be comfortable telling these stories to romantic interests in the future?

-Can any of these stories be told to help someone understand you better?

-Which story has had the biggest impact on your life?

-Have you ever told an embarrassing yet funny story about yourself and turned someone off? If so, was that person your type?

-Do you consider yourself someone who has a good sense of humor?

-Is a sense of humor important to you?

-Does your partner have to have the same sense of humor as you?

Exercise 4

Double (Standard) Your Pleasure, Double (Standard) Your Fun

Write out all the people that you have had a romantic physical experience with. Put their names in the list for the highest base you made it to with them. Each base is described below:

*First base: the first step in a sexual relationship involving making out or French kissing
*Second base: the second step in a sexual relationship involving heavy petting, feeling up or groping above the waist while making out either up the shirt or shirtless for both partners
*Third base: the third step in a sexual relationship involving the delivery of a handjob, fingering or oral sex
*All the Way: the act of having sex, vaginal or anal, with the intention of sexual pleasure and orgasm

First	Second	Third	All the Way
___	___	___	___
___	___	___	___
___	___	___	___
___	___	___	___
___	___	___	___
___	___	___	___
___	___	___	___
___	___	___	___

Thinking Points

-What are your requirements for physical intimacy?
-How far are you willing to go before being in a relationship?
-How many times did you go all the way without being in a relationship?
-Have you used a romantic experience to gain someone's affection or attention?
-If so, did it work?
-Which of the bases do you enjoy the most?
-Do you have more romantic physical experiences when you are single or when you are in relationships?
-Do you enjoy physical romantic experiences more when you are single or in relationships?
-What is your opinion of a woman simply wanting to experience a sexual encounter without any emotional attachment?
-What is your opinion of a man simply wanting to experience a sexual encounter without any emotional attachment?
-Do you believe the double standard is just?
-Have you ever been the victim of scrutiny from the rules of the double standard?
-If so, did that change the way you approached future romantic physical encounters?

Exercise 5
Easy as Attributes Before Characteristics

Write out all of your most important and defining personal attributes. Your attributes can be things you own, places you've gone, skills you have and physical features.

_____   _____

_____   _____

_____   _____

_____   _____

_____   _____

_____   _____

_____   _____

_____   _____

_____   _____

Write out a list of your characteristics. Characteristics are descriptions of who you are limited only to your character traits and personality. In the second column, list the exact opposite of your character list. Feel free to use a Thesaurus to capture the appropriate word.

Characteristics

Opposite Characteristics

_____   _____

_____   _____

_____   _____

_____   _____

_____   _____

_____   _____

_____   _____

_____   _____

_____   _____

_____   _____

_____   _____

_____   _____

_____   _____

_____   _____

_____   _____

_____   _____

_____   _____

_____   _____

Thinking Points

-Which list was harder to add to; attributes or characteristics?

-Are your characteristics what you want in a partner?

-Have you ever been with someone that has/had a similar characteristics list?

-Did you enjoy your time with that person?

-Have you ever been with someone that has/had an opposite characteristic list?

-Did you enjoy your time with that person?

-How many of the opposite characteristics list do you wish were a part of your character?

-Do you attract people with a list more like yours or more like that of your opposite?

-If you attract people more like your character, is this the kind of person you want to be with?

-If you attract people more like your opposite character, are you certain about which column you listed your characteristics? -If so, what about you still attracts these people?

Exercise 6
L is For…

Play the word search puzzle and look for five words that represent the ideas of being in a relationship that you have experienced or expect to experience. The words that you find first are said to be the ideas that you focus on the most.

```
T U T E C M Y E G D R F T S M U B I
K N V N I O Q C I N R E S R N R N I
C O E S E U M S A U I E G D U T G N
L H E M A M R P S M N V E N I H N S
V R E L S E L T R I I R I M A E I E
Y I I A S S R L L O S T I G C N N C
T T O P T A A E I T M D N N E O E U
Y R E L T I N R A F A I A I C I T R
P C O I E O N N R T L R S E N T S I
T O O P L N D G I A O U S E E C I T
M N W G P I C O N N B U F L I I L Y
L U X E N U N U G I B M E I T D P Y
S D U G R J S I U A A V E E A D E F
Y C N E T S I S N O C P L S P A Q N
N O I T C N U F S Y D H O N E S T Y
T S U R T N O I T A C I N U M M O C
U N H A P P I N E S S N O I S S A P
D O U B T D S S E N I P P A H C U G
N O I S U F N O C Y M A G O N O M O
B I S Y M P A T H Y J E A L O U S Y
Y T I R O I R P T C E P S E R G T B
T N E M T I M M O C R O M A N C E Q
```

ABUSE

ANGER

COMMITMENT

DISRESPECT

DYSFUNCTION

EQUALITY

FULFILLMENT

HAPPINESS

HURT

INSECURITY

INTIMIDATION

LIES

LONLINESS

MISERY

PAIN

PATIENCE

PRIORITY

ROMANCE

SYMPATHY

UNDERSTANDING

VIOLENCE

ADDICTION

CHEATING

COMMUNICATION

DOUBT

EMBARRASSMENT

FRUSTRATION

GIVING

HONESTY

IGNORANCE

INTIMACY

JEALOUSY

LISTENING

LOVE

MONOGAMY

PASSION

POWER

RESPECT

SUPPORT

TRUST

UNHAPPINESS

<u>Thinking Points</u>

-What words did you find first?

-Do these words represent your love life?

-Are you romantically involved a the moment?

-Have you experienced these ideas in your romantic past?

-Do you want to change any of the ideas you found?

-What words did you hope to find?

-How have you been improving yourself to experience the new words?

-Have you been in a relationship where these new words applied?

-Do you give these words to the relationship or do you expect them?

Exercise 7
E-VALUE-ATE Your Values

Carefully think about 5 of your core values. These ideas are things that you absolutely require with no exceptions. Next to each value, write down the name of the person that had the biggest impact on developing that particular value.

Value   Name

_____   _____

_____   _____

_____   _____

_____   _____

_____   _____

Thinking Points

-Did one person impact more than one value?
-Is this person anything like the type of person that you had the most successful relationship with?
-Have you ever gone against any of these values?
-Have you ever allowed someone to continuously go against your values?
-If so, is that value actually valuable to you?
-Which of these values is most important?
-When have you ever defended the more important values against someone that disagrees with the values' importance?

-Do your values match ideas from the word search exercise?

Exercise 8
Closed Mouths Don't Get Fed

Throughout your day, pay attention to the times you want something. Write down each time you ask for something that might put another person out of their way to get it done for you.

Thinking Points

-Did many of the things you ask for come from the same person?
-Do you rely on anyone else beside yourself?
-How long did you take before you asked for what you wanted?
-Were you nervous to ask? Why or why not?
-Why did you need that item or action?
-Did you receive it immediately or did you have to explain why you needed it?
-Did you explain why you needed that item or action without them asking for an explanation?
-If so, why?
-If not, do you normally get what you want?
-If you get what you want normally, do you think you get what you want because people know that you expect to?

Lyrical Memoirs

Sex

Language of Love

Quiero besar cada pulgada de su cuerpo hermosamente
succulento. Hola Senorita. Le nostre anime diventeranno
un quando facciamo le amore. Buongiorno principessa. Je
veux faire l'amour avec vous pour toujours. Bonjour
Mademoiselle. Don't worry about what I just said to you.
Actions speak much louder than words.
I could never say to you
All the little things that I want to do
There's not enough time in the world to say it all
One thing I know for sure
What you are looking for
You want me to stamp and sign my name along your walls
You wonder how I can tell
How do I know you so well
It's like I've already become your man
The way you licked your lips
It's like you made a wish
You spoke a language only we understand
Body language talk for me
Tell her what I want to do
Body language you must speak
Or I will have to talk for you
Don't say a word
Let my tongue talk to your curves
The only sound
Might be me struggling for air if I begin to drown
Our bodies will have conversations
Until yours gets to feel a sensation
Once I stroke and you squeeze
I'll spank and you scream
Bring me to my knees

With your sensual energy
Body language talk for me
Tell her what I want to do
Body language you must speak
Or I will have to talk for you

Follow my Lead

Hello young lady what's your name
Wrapped in my arms you ought to be
I bet you aren't looking for a man
But what does that have to do with me
I only want you here and now
We can leave later up to chance
Falling in love I can show you how
Tonight I just want to dance
With you baby
So that I can do to your body whatever you like
For me to do baby
On the dance floor intertwined in the moonlight
Like oooh baby
You know that I'm noticing
Your motion is poetry
That makes your body Maya Angelou
I hope that I can handle you
That's what I'm gonna see
I love that look locked in your eyes
I know that you can feel my energy
God told me that you'd be mine
From before your baby shower past your eulogy
I hear your body calling my name
You know that I have to answer back

Mine will do the same
I will burn down a mattress in the fires of passion
With you baby
I want you forever but I'm satisfied with tonight
You need to choose baby
If you want me too then for the rest of my natural life
I will pursue baby
If you give me a piece
You know that I'll want some more
No one else will have to know if I can get you all alone
On eternity's dance floor
Dance with me
You just have to take my hand to see
I can fulfill your fantasies if you dance with me
You're the only one I want tonight
You're the only one I need
Take a chance and take my hand
Follow my lead

A Good Time

I can't wait to get home to you
With all the nasty freaky things that we're gonna do
We won't be getting to sleep any time soon
We're about to break everything in this bedroom
Mami daddy's home so say hi with no clothes on
You better get ready soon and I need you to get ready to
Whisper to me what you want to do to me
Now that we're all alone
Take your time to say it right
We have all night long

I want to stay inside until the sun begins to rise
I guarantee tonight we're going to have a good time
Answer me this question
Can we make love through the entire weekend
What would do and what would you say
To get four play performed your way
If I lick it in a circular swirl
Until your toes begin to curl
I'll be sure to lick you under
Until almost all the pink is gone
The ice cream in the fridge
Will get jealous of what I'm eatin on
When I whisper to you what I want to do to you
Now that we're all alone
I promise to take the time to say it right
We have all night long
Look me in my eyes while I'm buried in your thighs
I guarantee tonight we're going to have a good time
Go get some water and let's take a shower
Then we'll come back for more
If the room is rockin and the cops come knockin
Leave them right at the door
I'm too busy strokin your legs gently open
I know you can take it
We fell asleep in the wet spot
You know it's the best spot
I'm passin out butt naked
You're too beautiful there's nothing I won't do to you
Now that we're all alone
I'll take the time to do it right
We have all night long
I will not close my eyes until I'm sure you're satisfied
I guarantee tonight we're going to have a good time
We should get to it because it's our time to do it

Now that we're all alone
We should take the time to do it right
We have all night long
This evening will be on our minds for the rest of our lives
I guarantee tonight we're going to have a good time

Great Flood

I love it when nature calls
Let your rain fall
If you ever had the chance
Would you make love
For forty days and for forty nights
Why don't you do your rain dance
Back it up on me until you feel like it's wrong
But you don't want to be right
I don't play those games
Between your thighs it looks like rain
That storm is not too much to handle so
Once I find two of every animal
I will make you flood the world
Follow me to another world
Where the rain won't fall down from the world
Heaven nor the underworld
Can stop from filling up the world
Strike me with your thunder girl
I want to dive right in and go under girl
You can get it whenever you want it girl
You run the world so flood the world
Know that I have enough wood
Enough to make you rock my boat

Watch me get you wetter
Than it ever got in the Bible
I'll make you feel so good
You'll be calling the Lord's name in vain
Bring your umbrella
I'm about to make you rain
Tonight we will need to take it slow
We still have a very long way to go
I'm just saying that I'm giving you warning
It's going to be raining until the morning
Follow me to another world
Where the rain won't fall down from the world
Heaven nor the underworld
Can stop from filling up the world
Strike me with your thunder girl
I want to dive right in and go under girl
You can get it whenever you want it girl
You run the world so flood the world
Swimmers and sharks become pedestrians to this ark
The motion in our ocean gives them the right of way
I cannot deny the way that I will try to find the way
To ride the high tide today
The upside down rainbow on your smiling face
Gives proof of what God should say
You can flood the ocean bays
With the same water that washes mine away
I can say that I can wait
But I am not afraid
To wade through the rains
That create the drip of your tidal wave
Rain is pouring and I'm exploring
My one and only girl
I want to drown in your juices with no excuses
Let me make you flood the world

Do you want to flood the world
It looks like rain

More than Sex

It's 12 o'clock and we're all alone
Let your nose smell the floras of my cologne
You do not know what we're about to do
You have never been with me so you don't have a clue
Let me tell you this will be unfamiliar
You might think you've had it good but I'm amazing
Please don't be discreet when we're between the sheets
It's about to get crazy
Ask yourself if you want to sweat
Ask yourself if you want to scream
Ask yourself if you want it so good that it's hard to breathe
I plan to lick you from the bottom up to the top
As long as I keep hearing you declaring not to stop
When I lift you up high into the air
That white stuff will light up my facial hair
Turn around and get on all fours
Until we suffer a rug burn on my floor
I bite you and you start scratchin
Our camera calls out ACTION
Don't be afraid to take the takes it takes to get this right
My sheets are soaking wet
We haven't even started yet
I think that we just might make ourselves a baby tonight
I love it so much that I'm begging for some of it
I want it so get on it until the sunrise in the morning
You need me this evening so let yourself receive me

Be sexy and impress me by coming here to get me
We'll be winding and grinding taking a trip to ecstasy
Receive it and believe it because this is more than sex to
me

Orgasms

Girl you're beautiful
I really want to get through to you
You don't know the nasty freaky things
I want to do to you
Get into our panties
More than both cheeks of your booty do
Call me cops and robbers
I will never stop pursuing you
If bad sex was a test I'm about to fail that
My train track through your tunnel derailed that
Give it to you in so many positions
We might wind up rewriting a Karma Sutra revision
I am your fantasy incarnate can't you sense it
Assault and battery on that ass might land me in prison
You can take three breaks before I'm halfway finished
I'll be your pacifier and you be my Maggie Simpson
I don't even need for you to make this decision
Whether or not you're ready for me to fire up my engines
Step on the pedal and wait another two or three instants
I will put it in you down the road from long distance
In my personal opinion subsequent to commencement
Pleasure will deliver you to alternate dimensions
To a world where birds go swimming and clouds go fishin
Let's try to start an orgy with our parallel renditions
Dicks rigid with clits slippin and slick lips splittin

The natural high you get will simply leave your body lifted
Lickin and kissin your skin has gotten my tongue twisted
But I promise not to stop until you tap out in submission
Decipher my diction
I need for you to listen would you please pay attention
The orgasms you've never had
Have now become my mission
I'll search for your G spot like I work in forensics
The way the sheets glisten
Shows that I found it with precision
It would have been harder to mention
Where your G spot isn't
I found so many I couldn't put the number in to a statistic
This prowess should be forbidden like Garden of Eden
apples
Now I need to confess my sins and your nookie is the
chapel
Let me use my stroke to paint the walls of your temple
I'll make a masterpiece inside you
My brush is not simple
When I'm done my work will convince me
You're the Vagican City with a Clitstine Chapel
I am Joshua Da Vinci
I want to tongue kiss your juicy lips
In the place with no sunshine
Leaving them so wet that they can extinguish the sunrise
Taking us back to dark skies
So that we can keep the freaky goin
Don't stop now until the kitchen is what we're sleepin on
Now your legs get gyratin and quakin until you feel it
Because I'm about to take it with my tool and power drill it
Bursting into laughter when you pass out right after
I'm the vagina assassin known as the orgasm master

Midnight Snack

It's late and I'm hungry but I don't want food
Yet there's nothing to your cookies that I won't do
I just have to know the ingredients of your recipe
I need for you to show them to me
With my face sticky I'll say more please
I won't stop eating your Twinkie until the morning
Come on let's go so that I can lick your bowl
Turn the oven on
Between the sheets we'll find the bakery
I'm curious to see what you might make for me
If it's creamy on the inside and a warm golden brown
I think you should let me guzzle it down
Pie eating should be in the Olympics
Let me eat that pizza deep dish
I'll earn a gold medal when I finish
Please feed me this it tastes just like a Resse's
More than one way to eat this leaving you speechless
Feed me
I'm going to get much more than just a taste
Feed me
Those juices are going to get all over my face
Feed me
I plan to lick that juice off of your plate
Feed me
It smells so good that I'm running out of breath
Feed me
It tastes so good I compliment the chef
Feed me
With no help you can feed me yourself
There is a party in my mouth and you're the only invited
I'm a messy eater so do not feed me in silence

My mother always told me never to play with my food
You told me that I have to so I will
My pulse pounding and your heart racin
Making little circles of suckin and tastin
Swallowin while I wallow in
The creamy deliciousness of your milk chocolatey lip kisses
Found not on your face but definitely on mine
Savoring the sweetness of your sensual secretions
My face is ready to go swimming
I can't wait thirty minutes after I eat
Your cherry is so sweet
Diabetes is a minor consequence to taste your tasty treat
I have no option but to devour you whole
This night will unfold even if neither of us told
Even though I still want the world to know
Lickin and kissin your skin has gotten my tongue twisted
I won't stop until you tap out in submission
Relinquish your apprehensions and inhibitions
Feed me my midnight snack
Are you hungry baby

Lyrical Memoirs

Love

Woman of my Dreams

We've never met each other before but I recognize you
What I have to say to you might sound a little crazy
I have lived a thousand lifetimes standing beside you
In this one we have a house, two cars, three dogs
And four pretty babies
To see you in real life makes me feel like I'm dreaming
You are so much more beautiful than I could ever imagine
This is love at first sight and I hope that you can feel it
When the world doubts that we can work this out
We know it happened
I don't need to go too long to figure out that I need you
Here and now I devote myself to you
So that you could be all mine
Even if you were to be paralyzed I would shower and feed
you
Through sickness of health with poverty's wealth
For all time
I had a dream and here you are
If you feel like I'm going too fast please let me know
I would never want to scare you off
Just give me a chance and you'll never let me go
Before I never saw you before I knew that I loved you
Every moment not by your side drives me crazy
Even after all these years I know you're the one who
After this son will have a house, two cars, three dogs
And four pretty babies

Cinderella

Once upon a time on a beautifully moonlit summer
evening in the far away kingdom of Los Angeles, CA I met
a girl. We talked and we danced and frolicked the night
away. I haven't been able to tell her, but it was after that
night that this girl to whom I am willing to give everything
changed my life forever...
We locked eyes from across the room
I was spellbound by the way that she moved
Everything about her was different
I never wanted our conversation to end
As we danced then things got weird
When I opened my arms and I opened my eyes
The girl I was dancing with disappeared like a real life
Cinderella
I looked around
Maybe she went to get some water
It's like nobody remembered
It's like nobody saw her
That's when I realized
The clock just struck a bell
Then the back door flew open
Before it ever even got to 12
I'll search high
I'll search low
I won't stop until I find her, no
There's nowhere I won't look
There is nowhere I won't go
I will travel the word
To find you and make you my girl
There is nothing I won't do
To spend the rest of my life with you
Wherever you are, whoever you are, that glass slipper that

you left behind was my heart. I know you are the perfect
fit. Your scent, your smile, your laugh, your touch, your
everything. I want to give everything to you. I need you to
live happily ever after. Yes you. My Cinderella…

Smile

One way to make your woman's sunrise
Is if you never let hers set
If you can make her feel like sunshine
Be sure that she will never forget
For some ladies feeling like they're beautiful
Can prove itself to be difficult
If a gentleman can pull out a chair and open a door
Keeping her happy is what her man is for
Tell her smile for me
You've got such a pretty smile to me
I know it might take a little while to be
Beyond the denial that we are all in pain right now
Smile for me because every man, woman and child can see
The sun rises in your eyes so clear the skies
Smile for me
Most men are so used to running from their feelings
We just need someone to listen sometimes
Only a lover can bring us to that healing
How about you sit him down and give it a try
When a woman tries to judge a man
About something she doesn't understand
She brings a pain that can build into rage and animosity
Say something she doesn't mean and then nobody is happy
Make him smile for you

Tell him you love it when he smiles for you
We act like it's not really our style to do
You already have so much to prove
If you can show him how
He will smile for you and bring a wedding and a child to
you
First you have to ease his hurtin and make certain
He smiles for you
We search our whole lives just to find someone to call our
own
To keep us smiling all the time so we never feel alone
I need more than a thousand words
To describe that beautiful smile of hers
When the world drives me crazy
It's her that I call to save me
It's never fake and it's not pretend
Through thick and thin until the end
If you see your lover start to frown
Sit your lover down
Tell them smile for me
It makes me happy when you're smiling
I know it's happy you desire to be
Sadness is so tiring so I want to scream out loud
Smile for me until you tire out a thousand cheeks
The sun will switch to the moon as long as you two
Smile for me

Believe Me

When I walked through the door
I told her I'd be home by one
It was already half past four

I promise I was so scared
When I turned on the lights
My lady was sitting right there
I asked why was she sitting in the dark like that
She wanted to sit inside of the way that her heart felt
Until I came back
I just couldn't believe I was dumb enough not to call
I had to tell her truth and come clean about it all
I was out with my boys at a club
There were women everywhere
Uh Oh
I told them all that I had a girl
They said they didn't care
Oh No
My mind was clouded and I thought about it
But I never cheated and I hope she believes it
I didn't want her furious with me
Because of simple curiosity
I know that TNA is TNT
For Y-O-U and M-E
I spent the time to make her want to be my wife
That's why she's the only girl that I need in my life
I know that girls go out just to have a little fun
But women are used to someone saying hi
It's easier to say that her man is the only one
That's why all the good men stay at home
It's the only way to leave the other girls alone
I was out with my boys at a club
There were women everywhere
Uh Oh
I told them all that I had a girl
They said they didn't care
Oh No

My mind was clouded and I thought about it
But I never cheated and I hope she believes it

My Angel

Lord, thank you. First you brought me life and then you brought me her. Everything I have, everything I have ever wanted and everything I am is because of her. I never thought that I would ever be able to love again. I was on a path of always doing wrong, never to do right again. Out of nowhere she came into my life and helped me see the light again. We have to experience pain before joy. We have to see rain before we can enjoy a rainbow. Sometimes we have to know danger before we can truly know what it is to feel safe. I can say that I know I'm safe in the arms of my angel. Amen.
I used to be lost with nowhere to turn
My life was in shambles on the path to crash and burn
I almost gave up but that's when I prayed
God send me a sign that I may see a brighter day
My angel bless me with your love
Save me with your touch my angel
Then I'll know that if I was to die today
I would die in your arms and you'd open your wings
So we could fly away
The gold in your eyes and the silk of your skin
Our first kiss you turned salvation out of sin
Now when I am judged and I make it through
I will tell St. Peter it was all because of you
My angel bless me with your love
Save me with your touch my angel
Then I'll know that if I was to die today

I would die in your arms and you'd open your wings
So we could fly away
You keep me warm in a world left so cold
God made you without destroying your mold
He watches you on his trophy shelf
Heaven is missing you but I want to keep you to myself
Around you moonlight is just sunshine in the dark
You make my life brighter when you shine as my morning
star
My angel bless me with your love
Save me with your touch my angel
Then I'll know that if I was to die today
I would die in your arms and you'd open your wings
So we could fly away

Eternity

I've been told I get too excited
How am I supposed to love you in silence
I appreciate what I've been through
All the time I spent alone is over with you
It's crazy and amazing
So highly exciting
You give to me the will to be
Will you live for me
Know that forever we'll be together
From dawn to the dusk until the dawn comes again
For all time
You will be all mine
Through losses and wins the thick and thin to the end
I think that you deserve

Way more than just the world you're my universe
Let me say that as your man
I will be there to hold you until time has no hands
I want you to hold on to
My love in spite of
What anyone might say you're all mine
For all time
Know that forever we'll be together
From dawn to the dusk and until the dawn comes again
For all time
You will be all mine
Through losses and wins and the thick and thin to the end
You and I could be so strong
I've wanted to ask you this for so long
I'm kneeling down on one knee with this ring
Asking will you marry me

Forever Yours

From the moment that I met you
I knew I'd never forget you
You are not only fine
You've got a beautiful mind
I had to know
How far this could go
If you give me the chance
I swear I'll be your man
Now every time that I look at you
It's like I'm staring at a statue
You're more beautiful than a goddess
That's just me being modest
I will never stop wanting you

Forever I will hold on to you
Your smile is brighter than the stars
I'm in awe of how beautiful you are
For all time
You will be all mine
Anybody that's not us
Will never have the power to stop us
Loving you is my way
To fight through lonely days
You should see what I have in store
I'll bring to you the universe and more
The fact that you desire me
Is simply inspiring
For a moment to hold you
There's nothing in the world that I won't do
You're all I need
You're more important than the air I breathe
Your heartbeat is my love song
When I'm with you nothing can go wrong
All I want to do is make you mine
I don't care if there's a snowstorm or volcano
If hurricane winds blow
I'll stand outside your window
Singing my love for you one note at a time
I think back to that one night
We spoke the moon into sunlight
I knew I had become right
Now I want to be your love life
My sweet we only get one life
I promise to get this one right
With me yours will be done right
I cannot control the future
I cannot change the past

But you are something I can put my hands on
I know that we can make it last
Home is where the heart lives
My heart is an open door
Close it behind you
I'm forever yours

Lyrical Memoirs

Fear

Only Skin Deep

Who is the fairest of all of the fair
That secret the mirror should keep
No matter the beast to look into the glass
This wolf sees itself as a sheep
Flawless exterior smiling and laughing
A princess to all of the land
If you should cut her to see if she bleeds
The knife will dissolve in your hand
She amputated the reaper's arm
Removed from him his scythe
She took the sandman's hourglass
Turned it on its side
With still beating bleeding hearts
Her moral fabric stained
A senseless masochistic victim's
Liquid crimson drained
Wanting of nothing but wanted by all
Fed is her vanity fuel
Unknown to all of her worshippers
She only painted the gold in her rules
Laws of the world are beneath her
Learning to run before able to crawl
Be our example for pride is the catalyst
Always preceding the fall

Get Out While You Can

Girl you're wasting your time
Leaving your heart on the line
You must be out of your mind

Wanting to stay with me
I know that you want romance
But if your heart wants to dance
Please get away take your chance
Could you escape from me
I don't think that you believe that I'm officially
The worst thing that has ever happened to you
That's why I say
Get away and far away
Hopefully today or whenever you're ready to
From the day I was born
I was not meant to be yours
To be completely sure you were warned
That was my top mission
Do you stay out of fear
Or is something wrong with your ears
Either you cannot hear
Or you do not listen
If you were a horse of course
I'm the rider in the saddle holding onto your reigns
I will use and abuse you refusing to lose you
And ever change
I was supposed to be
Like your shining star
But smoke and mirror with fire and flames
That's all that we really are
I wish that you could see and understand
I'm a faded picture perfect man
Get out while you can

Hate the Game

You can call me anytime even in the late night
When he doesn't hit it right
You just have to swallow your pride
You're asking me for presents and kissing me in public
I don't think you understand
Baby girl I am not your man
I'm not trying to hurt your feelings
I just want to make something clearer
If you want someone to love you
You'd better look in the mirror
We had a good run and had a whole lot of fun
It's not my fault you fell in love
You need to learn to control your heart
How am I the bad guy because I let us pass by
You don't need to ask why
You knew what this was from the start
You put me too high on your food chain
I might have to start to ignore you
I don't want to get you in trouble
Your husband and kids are waiting for you
Who do you think you are
Are you upset now or do you regret now
What you agreed to
You let it get this far
I know I said it so just you forget it
I do not need you
You have a husband and kids
He's asking questions but here's a suggestion
Stop calling him my name
What do you think this is
Don't hate the player you need to hate the game

Love's Lullaby

I can't imagine what was going through your mind
It's hard to breathe I can't believe
This is happening to me hmmmmm
What a perfect way to waste seven years of my time
I aim to be plain to see
This was a waste of history hmmmmm
I know the truth is all over you
I walked in the room to see you with some guy
Spreading your thighs to the sky
So tell me why do you cry
While I stand here and tell you goodbye
I heard you speak and I heard you cry
But I know you cheated and I know you lied
Don't say a word and don't even try
You murdered my trust and this is goodbye
I'm resting in pieces to love's lullaby
Why my dear are you standing here
Pack up your shit and go
The clock has struck so box it up
Get the hell away from me now
Girl you're just lucky
I didn't murder you both
I saw you fuck like I was nothing
Get your stuff and get out
Nothing you say will make it okay
Get out by today and let's not pretend
Like we'll try to be friends
This is my chance to take a stand
Girl this is truly the end
I heard you speak and I heard you cry
But I know you cheated and I know you lied

Don't say a word and don't even try
You murdered my trust and this is goodbye
I'm resting in pieces to love's lullaby

Did You Ever

I feel like a grain of pepper in a saltshaker
Left all alone dropped by a stone cold heart breaker
She made my life the first of my worst nightmares
Even though I fight tears I wish that she were right here
I want to make her smile but she's gone now
She flipped my world upside down
I cried myself a river that was bigger than the Nile
If I wallow in denial
I'll have to sit here for a while until I work it out
I knew something was wrong
From the moment you said that you needed to be alone
You told me over the phone when you got home
Like a sad love song
Your love for me was all gone for so long
My heart was on my sleeve and now it's bleeding
When we hung up I thought I was dreaming
I pinched myself because it just went too far
I realized this couldn't have been who you are
I gained a new perception
I sat and asked myself some simple questions
Did she ever love me
Did you
Did she ever want me
Did you
She would be kissing my lips and holding my hand
Talking marriage and children but then changed our plans

Out of nowhere she wanted to end
I figured the entire relationship was pretend
Pain is inspiration so that clarity I can snap into
What exactly will cryin and sentimental yappin do
The best thing to happen to you is all that you're attracted
to
You're the single worst thing they've ever had happen to
I never should have had to fear that
Take me back to the past
Give me my last seven years back
DO YOU HEAR THAT
Your reason was to be my wife
I used to be upset but now
Your lifetime became seasonal
All of our snow is meltin down
You said you loved me and I didn't doubt you
I stupidly assumed that I knew everything about you
You acted like a soul mate and I swore that I found you
My stomach cringed every moment I wasn't around you
Now I need to man up because though I stand tough
Being alone on stone cold linoleum
Makes a grown man tough
On that morning when I gloriously stand up
The television will be the only way you can stay in touch
I'm goin nuts because love was supposed to be enough
To fisticuffs with distance
In the instances that lonely struck
I guess I'm the fuckin duck for puttin trust in us
Discussin lust becoming love
When actually we were nothin but
I'm certain me hurtin was further from a concern to you
You just don't know how fervently
I was yearnin to murder you

Urgently learnin murderous urges I was turnin to
To burn you to the earth
And put the ashes in an urn or two
I would drop the vase of your remains
From a 40-story vertical
I wonder if I'm insane or if I'm dreamin
None of this changed
Until this bitch came with her sick games I believed in
Now it's in vain to feel this pain
Over this dame for leavin
Believe it
I need to breathe through these ruthless and couth less
Devil thoughts
To tape a hand grenade to your face
And pull the pin to set it off
But I'm a poet
FUCK YOU would have never said it all
They're metaphors
Why the fuck else would I have said it for
Yeah I know it's hella wrong
But I chased your ass for hella long
The one thing that I never saw
Is that I was never yours

Loved and Lost

I met a girl from Chicago
You'd swear she was a model
But I could not pretend
To be ready for love again
She looked at me and smiled
She said to stay a little while

The old me would think it could be
This is the woman of my dreams
Her middle name was Nikita
I said that it's nice to meet ya
She reached out for my hand
Asked me would I like to dance
My heart was not that strong
I hadn't been healing for that long
When I look back on that day
I let that woman walk away
Sometimes people in our lives
Try to give us good advice
No one except you knows what's going on
Some people think it's better to have loved and lost
Than never to have loved at all
Until they try and let time go by
One thing my friends say I must do
Is love and respectfully trust you
Tell me how many times
Should I let you cross the line
I wish that they could see
The ways that you have betrayed me
Then they would be on my side
I know that you and I was a lie
Red handed and still you said no
I knew it was time to let go
My pile of evidence
Makes your pleas irrelevant
I'm not satisfied
I don't believe you when you cry
That only tells me you're scared
Tears don't mean you care
Sometimes people in our lives

Try to give us good advice
No one except you knows what's going on
Some people think it's better to have loved and lost
Than never to have loved at all
Until they try and let time go by
It's cold and lonely all alone
Take it from me you will make it on your own
When you're freezing from the rain
When you can't take any more pain
Don't be shy and give it time
The sun will shine on the other side
Sometimes people in our lives
Try to give us good advice
No one except you knows what's going on
Some people think it's better to have loved and lost
Than never to have loved at all
Until they try and let time go by
If you have survived the most intense emotional, physical
and spiritual pain at the hands of someone else and you are
still alive to read this, remember this. If they bring you
pain, don't let them ever take your peace. I've been there.
I know there is someone reading this and going through
this exact same thing right now. Trust me… things get
better on the other side. When it hurts so much inside it
feels like you want to die… that's when you know you're
going to make it. Just hold on.

More

Do you ever think about the day I tried to propose
At that little restaurant all those years ago
I wanted to hear you say yes to feel like Christmas day

Now it's hard for me to say that I don't feel the same way
I'm just getting sick and tired of trying to impress you
Nothing is ever good enough no matter what I do
I want to make this work but I have to let you know
If you don't want me around then you need to let me go
I spend the time and pay the price to do all that I can
To keep you happy and make you smile as a better man
I took the steps and now my shoes and I don't have a soul
If you don't want me anymore tell me so I can be alone
It seems like everything you told me was a lie
You used to tell me that you wanted to be my bride
Plenty other women wait for this to end so I can choose
I give everything to you but I am still so confused
It's been seven years too long and I don't understand
How you gave me my kids with no ring for your hand
I've been around a long time and I know this game well
If you want me to yourself or not is still too hard to tell
If you can see our destinies joining intertwined
Obviously you don't need so many years to make your mind
You have lost so many points that I forgot the score
I will no longer be ignored you need to give me more

ABOUT THE AUTHOR

Joshua DuBois is a native of Inglewood, CA born on July 25, 1987. At 4 years old he recited a poem for his church entitled *Hey Black Child* and Joshua has had a passion for story telling ever since. He was enrolled in the All About Kids Acting Conservatory where he learned classical theatre and started his acting career. At the time, however, Joshua did not feel he was yet well rounded enough for film and television, so he went on a hiatus from acting to further develop his skills as an entertainer. While earning his Bachelor's Degree in Electrical Engineering from Southern University and A&M College, Joshua taught himself to play the electric guitar and piano, became a notable spoken word poet, learned gymnastics tumbling, joined a modeling troop, pledged a fraternity and performed in a heavy metal rock band. He firmly believes that a good storyteller can be anything, but a great storyteller can become everything so that he can personally connect with a wider audience from a variety of backgrounds. He has spent his entire life listening to, observing and counseling his friends, co-workers and family members in matters of romance from an empathetically rational state of mind. He is thusly very emotionally intelligent, boasting a deeply rooted compassion for the emotional needs of people in all walks of life. He coined the phrase "Josh of all trades" because he has worked his entire life to feed his need to be great at any- and everything he puts his mind to. He works daily to satisfy that need by always trying to entertain the world one audience at a time.